John Bird Sumner

Evangelical Archbishop

To the memory of

THE REVEREND GEORGE MALCOLM

1903–1989

John Bird Sumner

Evangelical Archbishop

Nigel Scotland

Gracewing.

First published in 1995

Gracewing
Fowler Wright Books
2 Southern Ave, Leominster
Herefordshire HR6 0QF

Gracewing books are distributed

In New Zealand by
Catholic Supplies Ltd
80 Adelaide Road
Wellington
New Zealand

In Australia by
Charles Paine Pty Ltd
8 Ferris Street
North Parramatta
NSW 2151 Australia

In USA by
Morehouse Publishing
PO Box 1321
Harrisburg
PA 17105 USA

In Canada by
Meakin and Associates
Unit 17, 81 Aurega Drive
Nepean, Ontario
KZE 7Y5, Canada

Cover design by Rafi Mohammed

The portrait of John Bird Sumner by Margaret Carpenter on the frontispiece is reproduced by kind permission of Eton College Collections.

Typesetting by Reesprint, Radley, Oxfordshire, OX14 3AJ

Printed by Cromwell Press, Broughton Gifford, Wiltshire, SN12 8PH

ISBN 0 85244 246 7

Contents

John Bird Sumner whilst Bishop of Chester

By courtesy of the Dean and Chapter of Chester and the Chester County Council Archives and Local Studies Service

Lambeth Palace London SE1 7JU

**FOREWORD BY THE ARCHBISHOP OF CANTERBURY TO
'JOHN BIRD SUMNER : EVANGELICAL ARCHBISHOP'
BY DR NIGEL SCOTLAND**

In its obituary to Archbishop Sumner the Times of 8 September 1862 stated that 'the late
Archbishop must be regarded as one of the best prelates that ever lived'. Others have judged
his achiepiscopate rather more harshly. Edward Carpenter, in his book 'Cantuar : The
Archbishops in their Office', summed it up in this way, 'His tenure of office had not been
distinguished'.

Dr Scotland's new biography gives us all the chance to re-examine those opinions. Archbishop
Sumner has always suffered from the twin facts that most of his private papers were lost and
that no one has ever attempted to write a full-length biography of him whether during the last
century or in this.

As an author Dr Scotland shows his own sympathy with much of what Sumner held dear,
whilst being far from sycophantic. In particular he underlines Sumner's significance as a
bishop and archbishop who took evangelism and mission seriously both in this country and
overseas. I commend this book to those interested in the development of the Church of
England in the first half of the last century and as an attempt to reassess the life of a man
whose portrait here at Lambeth still radiates the warmth, zeal and compassion which many of
his contemporaries knew well.

† George Cantuar

ARCHBISHOP OF CANTERBURY

Preface

In *Barchester Towers*, Anthony Trollope's sequel to *The Warden*, Eleanor Arabin shows her growing High Church tendencies by putting up a memorial window in the cathedral and, we are told, by assuming 'a smile of gentle ridicule when the Archbishop of Canterbury is named'.[1] The novel was published in 1857; the Archbishop of Canterbury was John Bird Sumner. Why should it have been fashionable in High Church circles to hold their ecclesiastical superior in disdain? The answer is that Sumner was an evangelical, and it was supposed by Anglo-Catholics that evangelicals possessed an inadequate grasp of the faith upheld by the Church of England. Evangelicals were thought to be 'Low Church', little better than Dissenters and entirely unfitted to provide the occupant of the see of Canterbury. Sumner, furthermore, had been a member of the judicial committee of the Privy Council that in 1850 declared George Gorham's rejection of baptismal regeneration an acceptable Anglican view. So objectionable was the decision that the redoubtable Henry Phillpotts, Bishop of Exeter, took the extraordinary step of excommunicating Sumner, his own metropolitan. Sumner was denounced by his ecclesiastical opponents, and it is their view of the man that has been handed down to posterity. He has commonly been treated as a disloyal Anglican and, though unexceptionable as a man, an unworthy Primate of All England. It has been left to Nigel Scotland to redress the verdict of history.

In this book Sumner is depicted as a kindly, learned and dignified figure altogether suited to his high office. Above all he is shown to have been a man of moderation. Like his mentor Charles Simeon of Cambridge, Sumner was consistently averse to taking up an extreme position because he was always too aware of the considerations on the other side of the question. He was no fierce partisan, eager to put down views he did not understand. If he was strongly opposed to the Tractarians who infused fresh vigour into the High Church tradition from the 1830s onwards, it was because he understood all too well that their teachings diverged from the received Protestant consensus of Anglicanism. He concurred with the younger evangelical theologian William Goode who, when criticising the Tractarian position in 1842, declared that he was 'the advocate of no particular party or system, but of the Church of England itself'.[2] Earlier on Sumner had formulated an attitude towards baptismal regeneration that both appealed to the Reformation fathers of the church and attempted to conciliate the less militant High Churchmen of a previous generation. At the time of the Gorham judgement he was not trying to eradicate a form of churchmanship with which he disagreed, but to show that the evangelicals had a legitimate place within the church. As a man brought up in the eighteenth century, he was in high degree an advocate of the Georgian ideal of toleration.

Sumner's sympathies extended beyond his own communion. Like other evangelical churchmen, he upheld theological convictions that created a bond with evangelical nonconformists. Together they believed that salvation came through the sacrificial work of Christ on the cross; that individuals must respond to the gospel in conversion; that Christians had an obligation to be active in spreading the faith and performing good works; and that the Bible was the supreme authority in matters of faith and conduct. Thus in 1857 Sumner invited Jabez Bunting, the venerable leader of Wesleyan Methodism, and Edward Steane, who was secretary of both the Baptist Union and the Evangelical Alliance, to Lambeth Palace, where they met a number of bishops. Such countenancing of ministers of other denominations aroused the ire of some High Churchmen, but to the Archbishop it was a natural expression of common Christian allegiance.[3] Nor did Sumner show the virulent form of anti-

Catholicism that disfigured much evangelical opinion in his day. In 1829 his maiden speech in the House of Lords as Bishop of Chester was a vindication of the right of Roman Catholics to share in the electoral franchise. Catholics, in his view, might be theologically mistaken, but that did not justify discrimination against them. He was even willing to contemplate the possibility of a Roman Catholic Prime Minister, an unusually liberal position for an early nineteenth-century churchman. He was a man who, alongside deep Christian convictions, held broad and generous sentiments.

Recent published work has demonstrated that evangelicals of Sumner's generation were in the vanguard of scholarship. Doreen Rosman has shown that they ventured far into almost every cultural sphere, and Boyd Hilton has argued persuasively that evangelical assumptions moulded discussion of social questions and economic policy.[4] While a schoolmaster at Eton, Sumner prepared two books that exerted a profound influence on his contemporaries. His *Apostolic Preaching Considered* (1815) was a telling theological work on the nature of the gospel. The other major book from his pen, *A Treatise on the Records of the Creation* (1816), examined the ways of God in the natural world and everyday human affairs. It therefore formed a significant contribution to science and to economic theory. There was nothing obscurantist about his views on the relation of religion and science:

> . . . the absurdity of supposing [he explains], that the literal interpretation of terms in Scripture ought to interfere with the advancement of philosophical inquiry, would have been as generally forgotten as renounced, if the oppressors of Galileo had not found a place in history.[5]

The brand of evangelicalism represented by Sumner was as remote from the fundamentalism of the twentieth century as it could be.

Sumner was one of the figures responsible for the resurgence of the Church of England in the early nineteenth century. During the eighteenth century, despite bright exceptions, the clergy had often not exerted themselves to gain a hold on the loyalties of the people and church attendance had fallen away. By the middle of the nineteenth century, largely as a result of the impact of the evangelical revival, there was a new vibrancy in the Church. 'Then', remarked the evangelical Anglican journal *The Record* in 1850 about the mid-eighteenth century, 'all was dead — now all is life.'[6] Sumner played his part in the hardest location of all — the diocese of Chester that included most of the heavily industrialised county of Lancashire. There he stimulated church building to cater for the new industrial workforce and prompted his clergy into conscientious visitation of their flocks. He also participated in the worldwide expansion of Anglicanism, supporting the Society for the Propagation of the Gospel as well as the evangelical Church Missionary Society and advancing the creation of colonial bishoprics. He deserves recognition as one of the creators of the modern Anglican communion at home and abroad.

The gravestone of John Bird Sumner in Canterbury Cathedral is extraordinarily laconic, recording no more than his dates of birth and death. It symbolises the way in which he has been allowed to languish in obscurity. Hitherto it has been difficult to gain more than a passing acquaintance with the man, for he has normally been thought fit only for the 'gentle ridicule' of Eleanor Arabin. A biography of Sumner is long overdue, and it is extremely welcome that Nigel Scotland has seen the gap and filled it. The author, who has already written illuminatingly on Primitive Methodists, a very different section of the diverse evangelical world, has put a great deal of research into this book. The result is a clear picture of an eminent man remarkable for his moderation. The first evangelical Archbishop of Canterbury now has a fitting memorial.

D. W. Bebbington

Stirling, September 1995

Notes

1. Trollope Anthony, *Barchester Towers* [1857] (London, Oxford University Press, 1925), p.505.
2. Goode William, *The Divine Rule of Faith and Practice* [1842] (3 vols, second edition, London, John Henry Jackson, 1853), p. xxxiv.
3. Payne E.A., *The Baptist Union: A Short History* (London, Carey Kingsgate Press, 1958), p. 83.
4. Rosman Doreen, *Evangelicals and Culture* (London, Croom Helm, 1984). Hilton Boyd, *The Age of Atonement: The Influence of Evangelicalism on Social and Economic Thought*, 1785–1865 (Oxford, Clarendon Press, 1988).
5. Sumner J.B., *A Treatise on the Records of Creation* (fifth edition, 2 volumes, London, J. Hatchard, 1833), 1, p. 325.
6. *The Record*, 3 January 1850, p. [4].

Introduction

John Bird Sumner was born in 1780, and by the time of his death in 1862, he had not only become the first Archbishop to be an avowed evangelical, but had also witnessed at first hand, and in a position of authority, the extraordinarily crucial changes that occurred due to Britain's rapid industrialisation and urbanisation. Somewhat surprisingly, no standard Life and Letters of John Bird Sumner was produced by any member of his immediate family circle as was the case with most Victorian prelates. Even more remarkably in the century that followed no subsequent biography of Sumner has been attempted. In recent years all that has been written about this remarkable figure are an MA thesis by E.R. Moore covering his Chester Episcopate, and one or two pages in diocesan histories and surveys of Victorian prelates. This study is therefore the first attempt at a full biography of Sumner.

Those who have however taken the time to assess his achievements cannot but have been struck by the fact that Sumner is a much overlooked Victorian Churchman, and in many ways a much underestimated Archbishop of Canterbury. A gifted academic, he had in his earlier years produced a number of scholarly and pastoral books, the most significant being *Apostolic Preaching Considered* (1815) and a *Treatise on the Records of Creation* (2 Volumes, 1816), the latter a serious attempt to grapple with social theory in the light of biblical principles.

In his years as Bishop of Chester Sumner proved an outstanding pastor and a gifted administrator who grappled effectively with a huge diocese which included the Lancashire cotton towns and the sprawling conurbations of Liverpool and Manchester. In the early years of the nineteenth century the Church of England had not been awake to the problems associated with the rapidly increasing industrial population.

There was a desperate need for new church buildings and increased accommodation. Sumner energetically set about the task of making good this deficiency. In 1839 he gave an account of the church building programme which had been undertaken in Chester diocese since he had become its bishop. In all he had consecrated 161 churches with 20,047 sittings in Cheshire and 99,037 sittings in Lancashire.

Sumner became Archbishop of Canterbury in 1848 on the death of William Howley. Commenting on Sumner's elevation the *Manchester Guardian* newspaper described him as 'the prominent advocate of Evangelical views'. Nevertheless his archiepiscopate was marked by mild and statesmanlike policies and an almost total lack of factionalism. In all respects Sumner demonstrated over his years in office that he had indeed been the right man for what proved to be fourteen years of crisis for the Church. One of his first acts was to consecrate Renn Hampden as Bishop of Hereford when almost all his colleagues on the bench had expressed their opposition to his appointment. This was immediately followed by the Gorham controversy in which Henry Phillpotts, Bishop of Exeter, refused to institute George Cornelius Gorham to a living in his diocese because of his view on baptismal regeneration. The case, which was even discussed in Parliament, proved in the end a triumph for the evangelical and low Church cause and resulted in a further secession of Anglican clerics to the Roman Church.

In 1850 the way was opened for the restoration of the Roman Catholic episcopal hierarchy in England. It was greeted by a nationwide storm of protest. This was followed by lengthy debates over proposals to revive the Upper House of Convocation as a final court of appeal in doctrinal matters. The close of Sumner's primacy was marked by struggles over the burial laws and Church rates and by the publication of two controversial books, Charles Darwin's *Origin of Species* in 1859 and an all-Anglican volume entitled *Essays and Reviews* in 1860. The latter created doubts about the inspiration and reliability of scripture among clergy and laity alike, whilst the former posed searching questions for those who viewed the world as being entirely God's creation.

The years of Sumner's archiepiscopate were a time when the world-wide Anglican Communion was growing very rapidly with the expansion of the British colonies. This situation demanded that the primate make many important decisions about the government of the colonial Churches and their relationship to Church of England missionary agencies. These decisions would have lasting consequences for the future of the Anglican Church in the decades that were to follow. In addition many key appointments to the overseas episcopate had to be made by Sumner during his period of office, and each one called on him to achieve a fair balance between the needs of the Church at home and overseas.

In all these several aspects Sumner showed himself to be a wise and temperate leader who held firmly to the credal faith and the protestant teaching of the Thirty-Nine Articles. He was remembered by all who knew him for his straightforward but firmly held beliefs, as well as for his gracious and dignified dealings with representatives of all parties and persuasions.

Acknowledgements

I should like to acknowledge the kindness of various owners of manuscripts who have allowed me access to Sumner's letters and papers. Mr. Cecil Sumner, the last surviving descendant of Bishop Charles Richard Sumner, John Bird's younger brother, gave me valuable information about the family. The Warwickshire record office helped me to locate material relating to Sumner's early years at Kenilworth and the Cumbria Record Office also supplied documents relating to the family circle. Both the Chester and the Canterbury diocesan record offices were extremely helpful in finding and making diocesan records available to me. Lambeth Palace Library kindly afforded me the benefits of the Archbishop's Act Books and other relevant manuscripts. The Department of Palaeography and Diplomatic at Durham University provided me with copies of Sumner's correspondence with the 3rd Earl Grey. This shed much valuable light on Sumner's dealings with the Colonial Church. Both the Bodleian Library at Oxford and the British Library in London proved to be mines of valuable information. The *Journal of Ecclesiastical History* very kindly advertised on my behalf for information concerning John Bird Sumner. I also benefited a great deal from the Locker collection which is in the possession of the Huntington Library, San Marino, California. Canon Michael Hennell formerly principal of Ridley Hall Cambridge, Dr David Bebbington, reader in history at the University of Stirling, Professor A.M.C. Waterman of the University of Manitoba and Mr Jeffery Turner all kindly gave me help and encouragement at various points along the way. I am also grateful to the Cheltenham and Gloucester College of Higher Education for allowing me sabbatical leave during the summer terms of 1988 and 1991. Finally, I am greatly indebted to Mrs Shirley Fiddimore for deciphering and word-processing an untidy manuscript, and to Meg Davies for her expert compilation of the Index.

Nigel Scotland

1

The Early Years

John Bird Sumner was born in February 1780, the first[1] child
of the Revd Robert and Hannah Sumner. The Sumner family
had for many years been closely identified with Eton. Robert's
father, John Sumner, was first Lower Master and then Headmaster of Eton and Canon of Windsor. He subsequently moved
on to be Provost of King's College, Cambridge, Eton's senior
and affiliated organisation. Robert's elder brother, Humphrey,
was an assistant master at Eton, following in his father's footsteps by becoming Provost of King's. A cousin, Robert Carey
Sumner, was also an assistant master at Eton and afterwards
Headmaster at Harrow.[2]

John Bird's father was born in 1748 and baptised in the
College Chapel which also served as the parish church. He was
admitted to King's College at the age of 17 as a scholar from
Eton. He received a BA in 1771 and an MA three years later.
He remained at King's as a fellow until 1774 when he left the
University to become Vicar of Kenilworth and Stoneleigh in
Warwickshire.[3]

It is not altogether clear how Sumner came to be instituted
to the living of Kenilworth, the advowson of which was held
by the Crown and the Lord Chancellor.[4] It may simply have
been through Eton contacts. The College was a royal foundation
and Robert's father's contacts at Windsor may well have brought
him to the notice of the right people. After five years' residence
in Kenilworth Robert Sumner married Hannah Bird whose
father, John Bird, had evidently been a person of some note in

1

the locality. The following inscription is affixed to the south wall of Kenilworth Church.

Near this place
Lye interred the Remains of John Bird, Esq.,
Alderman of the city of London,
Who departed this Life, on 18th October, 1772
in the 39th year of his age.
His afflicted widow Judith Bird
Has caused this monument to be erected
As a memorial
of their conjugal affection
and of her irreparable loss.

Despite dying at the comparatively young age of 39, John Bird was clearly a man of some distinction. He must have risen very quickly through the ranks of City government because by the time he was elected a Liveryman of the Goldsmiths' Company on 27 April 1770, he was already an Alderman for Bassishaw Ward. On 22 February 1771 John Bird was elected to the Court of Assistants of the Goldsmiths' Company. However, he died the following year and so never had the opportunity of serving as Sheriff or Lord Mayor.[5]

The Bird family had close links with the Wilberforces. Hannah Bird and William Wilberforce were first cousins and the two families enjoyed a long and fairly close relationship.[6] This was particularly evident in the case of Charles Sumner and Samuel Wilberforce and to a lesser degree in the case of John and Samuel.

Robert Sumner appears to have been a quiet and conscientious incumbent, and the parochial accounts appear to have been carefully kept. One example of this can be seen in the *Poor Rate Book* for the years 1784–95, which shows many entries in Sumner's own immaculate and clear hand. The great majority of baptisms, marriages and burials were conducted by Sumner himself, and it is clear he was no absentee parson depending on the services of a curate to perform the humble tasks of attending to the needs of the poor and performing the occasional offices.

During their years at Kenilworth the Sumners had several children. Robert was born the year following John Bird, but died in 1804 shortly after taking his degree at Cambridge.[8] Charles Richard, who later became bishop of Llandaff and Winchester, was born in 1790 and Henry Humphrey followed in 1792.[9] A sister, Maria, who was born in 1794,[10] later married the Revd Dr William Wilson, a fellow of The Queen's College Oxford who became Vicar of Holy Rood, Southampton, a Canon of Winchester and one of the founders in 1865 of the Evangelical Church Association which was established in an effort to counteract the later ritualistic extravagances of the Oxford Movement and the Cambridge Camden Society.[11]

Apart from the fact that he purchased two cottages in the High Street near the church from John Richards for the sum of £60 in 1787,[12] the parish records yield no further information about Robert Sumner. The main local newspaper of the period *The Coventry Mercury* gave only scant coverage of Kenilworth affairs. It would appear that at some point in the autumn of 1801 the incumbent of the parish took sick with a fever of some kind. After November of that year the entries in the baptismal register are no longer in the name of Robert Sumner and he may well have removed to London in an effort to get better medical care and attention. *The Coventry Mercury* in its issue of 18 October 1802 carried the following short notice of his death: 'Died on Sunday night in Weymouth Street, Portland Place, London, after a lingering illness, most sincerely regretted by his family and parishioners, the Reverend Robert Sumner, Vicar of Kenilworth and Stoneleigh, near this city'.[13] George Sumner, John Bird's nephew and the son of his younger brother Charles, later penned the following lines.

> Their father was a quiet, earnest country clergyman of small means, who died in 1802, when J.B. Sumner was twenty two, and R.C. Sumner was twelve years of age, leaving also two other sons of the ages of ten and twenty one years respectively.[14]

It is difficult to be sure as to the precise nature of the religion which was lived and preached in Kenilworth parsonage, but it is quite likely to have been influenced by the growing evangelical movement of the latter years of the eighteenth century. Kenilworth itself was touched by Methodist revivalism[15] and Hannah's cousin William Wilberforce had experienced his evangelical conversion in 1785.[16] It is difficult to conceive of his not sharing his new-found faith within his close-knit family circle. Certainly we know from extant letters that Hannah Sumner corresponded with William Wilberforce on family matters.[17] It is probable that John Bird received his earliest instruction at home in Kenilworth rectory before following the family tradition of being been sent away to Eton where his uncle, Humphrey Sumner, was an assistant master.

The Eton of the 1790s could be a fairly harsh place. The hours of study were long, floggings were frequent and the social life of the 'oppidans' was controlled by the celebrated Eton dames who had a reputation for strictness. The Head Master was Dr George Heath about whom there is only scant information. It is possible that Heath was somewhat deficient in vigour and lacking in discipline since school numbers fell by more than a hundred during the decade he was in office.[18] It is therefore likely that there was more than an element of truth in the complaints in the *Gentleman's Magazine* of 1798 about the low tone of morality in the school. What little religion there was in the institution was clearly minimal, dry and formal. The only religious instruction in the days when John Bird was a pupil in the school was the requirement to learn a few verses of the Greek Testament by heart on Sunday in order to say them on Monday morning. It was not the custom to explain or help the boys to understand what it was that they had learnt by heart!

Sumner evidently survived the experience—indeed much of it must have been to his liking, for after only a short time away at University he was to return to Eton as an assistant master. The records of the College have left us a few illuminating anecdotes that cast some light on Sumner's years at Eton. Cust recounts what appears to be a well substantiated story of 'Sumner's flirtation with the fair Martha at Spier's'.[19] Martha, it seems, worked at the Eton Sock Shop and the poet Shelley who was one of John Bird's contemporaries, spoke of her as 'the loveliest girl I ever saw, and I loved her to distraction.'[20] Sumner had the distinction of representing the school in the first cricket match ever to be played against a local club. The opposition was the nearby Oldfield side which they beat easily. Sumner was one of the bowlers.[21] It is quite likely that he would also have played the previous year in the first recorded public-school cricket match against Westminster which took place on 25 July 1796 on Hounslow Heath. There is no surviving record of the Eton side on that occasion, but it was comprehensively beaten!

John Bird left Eton in 1798. He was the first of his year and went up on a scholarship to King's College, Cambridge, where his uncle, Humphrey Sumner, was Provost.

Among the fellows of King's at this time was the celebrated Charles Simeon (1759–1836) who had undergone his evangelical conversion in the spring of 1779. He was to become both the national leader of the evangelical party in the Church of England, and the most influential Christian figure in the University for more than forty years. Simeon was a man of great grace and charm who soon endeared himself to the Provost of King's and this led to his appointment as the College Dean of Divinity. He was now placed in a position to exercise great influence particularly over the lives of the undergraduates and more junior members of the College.[22] It led to Simeon starting weekly tea parties to discuss the Christian faith in his rooms at King's every Friday night and, in addition, a sermon class for those who were studying divinity or considering the possibility of ordination. Over the years both these gatherings were attended by large numbers of undergraduates. Many embraced Simeon's evangelical faith and became active Christians at home or went out to serve on foreign mission fields.[23]

Like many others of his generation Sumner was touched by the influence of Charles Simeon[24] and became a convinced 'evangelical'. Indeed Simeon's example had a lasting effect on Sumner's care for the poor during his years as a master back at Eton College, and may well have contributed to his later pastoral zeal as Bishop of Chester in the 1820s and 1830s. Sumner's younger brother Charles was also much influenced by Simeon, as is evidenced by extant correspondence.[25]

Sumner's years at Cambridge were marked by academic distinction. He won the Sir William Browne medal for the Latin Ode in 1800 and added the Hulsean Divinity prize in 1802. He graduated Bachelor of Arts and was briefly a fellow of his College until the time of his marriage with Marianne Robertson in 1803. Later, in 1828, Sumner was awarded the degree of Doctor of Divinity.

By the time John Bird left the gracious surroundings of his College on the banks of the river Cam, the habits of study and the religious convictions which were to influence and shape his future career were firmly established. Sumner was a University prizeman whose disciplined academic routine enabled him to devote long hours to reading and writing, which resulted in the publication of more than forty works during his life. Clearly Sumner was one of the most fertile authors ever to hold the primacy of all England. Yet for all that, because of the commitments of his office he did not have sufficient time or energy to establish fully a reputation as an independent thinker. Most of his later treatises were not primarily academic and scholarly, but were rather practical and pastoral works which related to the office and tasks of the Christian ministry. In a parallel way, although Sumner left the University as a convinced Simeonite 'evangelical', he was never regarded as an aggressive hard-line party man. He did what the *Saturday Review* termed 'party work',[26] but it was largely through private rather than public channels. He was a man who all his life was deeply attached to his own family circle, spending time particularly with his mother at Milford, and his younger brother Charles and sister Maria.

Away from his own kin he numbered among his close friends the Simeonite evangelicals Henry Venn, Henry Raikes, and William Marsh. Indeed the latter two remained close associates of his until the day he died. In later years one of Sumner's great delights when Archbishop of Canterbury was to make the short journey from Addington to Beckenham, to converse with Marsh and share in the worship and ministry of his church.[27]

It was with these credentials that John Bird arrived back at his old school in 1803 to serve as an assistant master. He was to work first under Dr Goodhall and later under the celebrated John Keate.

Notes

1. *Baptismal Register Parish of Kenilworth*, Warwick County Archives DR/108/4 entry for 25 February 1780.
2. See Benson A.C., *Fasti Etonenses: A Biography of Eton* (London, Simpkin, Marshall & Co., 1899), p. 273 *et passim*.
3. Venn J., *Alumni Cantabrigienses*, Vol. 6, p. 83.
4. Pugh R.B., *A History of Warwick* (OUP, 1951), p. 141.
5. See Beavan A.B., *The Aldermen of the City of London*, Vol. 1 (1908), p. 200. See also City of London Freedom Admissions Archives, ref. CF1/969.
6. See Moore E.R., *John Bird Sumner Bp. of Chester 1828–48* (unpublished MA thesis, University of Manchester, 1976) p. 3.
7. See Parish of Kenilworth (Warwickshire County Archives) *Rate Book 1784–1795*, DR296/30.
8. *Kenilworth Baptismal Register*, Warwick County Archives DR/101/5, 12 August 1781.
9. *Ibid.*, 11 December 1792.
10. *Ibid.*, 24 April 1794.
11. See *Dictionary of National Biography* entry for the Revd Dr William Wilson (1783–1873).
12. Kenilworth Parish Records *Deeds of Two Cottages sold to the Rev. Robert Sumner 1787*, DR 189/15/1–8.
13. *Coventry Mercury* 18 October 1802. See also *Gentleman's Magazine* 1802, Vol. LXXII pt. 2, p. 1066.
14. Sumner G., *Life of R.C. Sumner DD Bishop of Winchester* (Murray, 1872), p. 2.
15. Ashwell, R., *Life of the Right Reverend Samuel Wilberforce*, Vol. I (London, J. Murray, 1880), p. 82.
16. See Pollock, J., *Wilberforce* (Berkhamsted, Lion, 1977), p. 35.
17. See for example MS Wilberforce C3 folio 127 Bodleian Library.
18. Sterry W., *Annals of King's College and of our Lady of Eton Beside Windsor* (London, Methuen, 1908), p. 203.
19. Cust L., *A History of Eton College* (London, J.C. Nimmo, 1881), p. 129.
20. *Ibid.*, p.169.
21. Anon, *Etoniana Ancient and Modern Being Notes and Traditions of Eton College* (William Blackwood & Sons, Edinburgh, 1845), p. 174.

22. See for example Carus W. (ed.) *Memoirs of the Life of Charles Simeon MA* (London, Hatchard, 1848), p. 64 *et passim.*

23. For a description of these see *ibid.*, p. 452

24. Atkinson, J.A., *A Memoir of the Revd Canon James Slade MA* Vicar of Bolton (1892), p. 2. See also *The Record* 8 September, 1862.

25. See Moule H.C.G. *Charles Simeon* (London, Inter-Varsity Fellowship, 1956), p. 49.

26. *The Saturday Review* 13 September 1862.

27. Marsh, *The Life of the Rev. William Marsh* (London, Hatchard & Co., 1867), p. 371.

2

Eton:

Schoolmaster & College Fellow

At some point in 1802 before he had received his BA degree John Bird returned to the school which he had left only four years previously, this time to take up a position as an assistant master.[1] He remained in this post for fifteen years until his election as a Fellow in 1817. His first year at the school brought two other new responsibilities; he was ordained on 6 March 1803 by the Bishop of Salisbury and later in the same month he married Mary Ann Robertson.

Sumner was commended to the Bishop of Salisbury by his uncle Humphrey Sumner, Provost of King's College, together with the Vice-Provost and two others of the fellows[2]. He subscribed to the Thirty-Nine Articles of the Church of England and to the three articles of the Thirty-Sixth Canon on the 5 March[3] and was duly made deacon the following day along with five others in the parish church of New Windsor[4]. Sumner was later priested in 1805, also by the Bishop of Salisbury[5].

On 31 March 1803 John Bird married Mary Ann Robertson the daughter of George and Anne Robertson. George Robertson was a captain in the Royal Navy and had been offered a knighthood by George III for his conduct in the battle of the Dogger Bank in 1781. His wife Anne was the daughter of Francis Lewis of New York, formerly of Llandaff.[6] Robertson came originally from Edinburgh but he and his wife settled for some years in Kenilworth where they were acquainted with John Bird's father the Revd Robert Sumner. Indeed he baptised

Marianne's distinguished younger brother Thomas Campbell
Robertson at Kenilworth parish church in November 1789.[7]
Captain Robertson died in 1791 and later the same year his wife,
Anne, moved to Edinburgh in order to take care of Thomas'
schooling.[8] She evidently retained her links with Kenilworth
and it was in this way that John Bird must have met Mary Ann
on a number of occasions possibly during the University vaca-
tions. John and Mary Ann were married at the parochial chapel
of St Mary, Walcot, Bath on 31 March 1803.[9] 'Marianne' who
was 22 years of age at the time of the wedding was by this time
resident in Walcot parish and it is likely that she either had a
position in one of the many large households of the parish or
that she was living with relatives. The latter is possible since
the marriage was solemnised by the Revd Love Robertson
(1765–1841) who also stood as bondsman for the marriage
licence. Love Robertson was in later years Vicar of Bridstow
in Herefordshire and a prebendary of Hereford Cathedral from
1804 to 1841.[10]

John Bird's years as a young schoolmaster appear to have
been fairly quiet and uneventful. His time must have been
largely spent enjoying his young wife's company and in pro-
viding for the needs of his rapidly growing family. Their first
child, Maria, was born in 1806 and seven other daughters were
to follow during the period of their residence at Eton. There
were moments of sadness such as when their third daughter,
Caroline, died after only two months in February 1811, but they
were consoled in the birth of twins in 1816, one of whom they
named Caroline.[11] The Sumners later had two sons who were
born at Mapledurham rectory. John Henry Robertson Sumner
was born in 1821 and in later life became rector of Ellesborough
in Buckinghamshire and Robert George Moncrieff Sumner
who was born in 1823 trained and practised as a barrister.

John Bird's tenure as an assistant master at his old school
must have been something of a sadness to him as the school
continued to be marked by a harsh and sometimes brutal
environment in which there was little or no opportunity for him
to share his simple faith in Christ with boys in his care. According to William Gladstone who was a pupil at the school in the

1820s, 'the actual teaching of Christianity was all but dead and John Bird Sumner was practically debarred from saying a word about God to his pupils'.[12] Sir John Patterson substantiated this claim asserting that Sumner himself spoke of his duties as an Assistant Master as a 'hateful trade'.[13]

Eton College had originally been established by Henry VI in 1441 by Royal Charter as a monastic institution for training poor scholars. All were to receive first tonsure at the proper age and were required to leave Eton at the age of eighteen unless their names had been placed on the roll of the older sister institution at King's College which Henry had also founded in Cambridge. After the Reformation, the College was organised on more Protestant lines and came to have a body of seventy poor scholars (and sixteen choristers) with about seven clerical fellows to instruct them. In addition, from the time of the Reformation a school began to develop in association with the College.

By Sumner's time the teaching of the boys (oppidans) and the scholars was almost entirely in the hands of the Headmaster and a staff of assistant masters. The Provost and fellows acted in a purely advisory and administrative capacity and spent their time in academic pursuits and in parochial preaching and pastoral work. Eton College Chapel was also the local parish church and provided worship for both the boys and the parishioners, many of whom were tradespeople or agricultural labourers. The Provost was to all intents and purposes Vicar of the parish of Eton and, together with the Eton College fellows, he was responsible for leading the services and preaching. Most of the fellows seem to have been dull and rather uninspiring individuals. A Colleger during the second decade of the nineteenth century wrote of the Sunday morning services as being 'intolerably long as was the custom of the age'.[14] He continued:

> They were mumbled and jumbled by old men with weak smothered voices; not one of which could be heard except by those immediately under them....[15]

The same pupil added that 'the sermons delivered by John Bird Sumner, after his promotion to a Fellowship, came as partial relief.'[16] Needless to say in the absence of any spiritual reality, the behaviour of the boys in the College Chapel often left much to be desired. On Sundays there were only four masters on duty and over five hundred boys to contend with[17] and behaviour was therefore often bad. The Revd C.A. Wilkinson who was a pupil in the early years of the nineteenth century recorded his own memories of Eton Chapel.

> The authorities themselves were not attentive. They could not expect us to be so. The clergyman and the clerk were only attentive to one thing, as to how they could rattle on, and dovetail Psalms and responses in, and get over the whole, including two lessons in about twenty minutes.[18]

In 1809 Dr John Goodhall was succeeded as head master by the under master, the celebrated John Keate who remained in office for 25 years. Keate who was a capital scholar was an extraordinary man by any standards. Although little more than five feet in height he had a noble voice which he modulated with great skill and he was renowned for 'very severe' discipline. Flogging was frequent during his period of office.[19] On one occasion Keate mistook a form master's list of boys who wanted to be considered for Confirmation as a flogging list. In spite of all protestations he flogged the boys there and then.[20]

John Bird's younger brother, Charles, was just on the point of leaving the school when Keate was appointed. A somewhat amusing letter written by him to his friend, John Patterson, has survived. It gives us some interesting insights into the way in which school business was conducted.

> As I think that you must by this time be safely landed in the wool-pits, take my dear Patty, some account of the various changes and chances which have taken place in the last four weeks. Of course the papers have shown how Goodhall is appointed Provost, how he has kissed, how he has retained his canonry, how—but all the other acts that he did, are they not written in the *Gazette* of December 15?...
>
> The canvas for the place of under master was hot—Thackeray, Carter, Drury and Yonge.... My brother canvasses strongly for Thackery... about three days ago their united efforts were successful. This will suit well with his weak state of health, for

though the business is if possible more than that of Assistant, yet it is lighter and less head work.

... Yonge is to come into the Upper School, being hand in glove with our supreme Keate.... Such is the state of things here, and it is altogether so unpleasing a prospect that I am very impatient to free myself from all the bore of verses and lyrics.[21]

By all accounts Sumner went about his business in a gracious and conscientious manner and he seems to have been universally popular with the boys. W. Sterry who was a pupil during Sumner's time as a master described him as 'the most popular of tutors'.[22] The boys nicknamed him 'Crumpet Sumner' on account of his complexion.[23] A.C. Benson afterwards wrote of Sumner in these years that 'he was a man of extraordinary self-restraint and method, regulating the employment of his time, his money, his hours of sleeping, eating and exercise by the strictest rules.'[24]

During his years as an assistant master Sumner divided his time between his family, the school, parochial work and writing projects. Besides caring for his clutch of growing young daughters, John Bird and Mary Ann had the responsibility of keeping a caring eye on his younger brother Charles. Ten years his junior, Charles arrived at Eton shortly before the time their father died. Their mother was left to care for their several brothers and sisters out of only limited resources with the result that Charles was forced to give up his private study. Henceforward he contented himself with a shelf in the Long Chamber and took his breakfast and tea in his brother's house.

Out of school hours John Bird devoted much time to visiting the sick and poor in and around Eton and Windsor.[25] In that service he was without doubt inspired by the ministry of Charles Simeon who about the year 1788 had begun the systematic care and visitation of the poor in and around Cambridge.[26] In the early days he actively involved himself in this work; later however he put the organisation into the hands of others. He established a number of different districts with thirty male and female visitors who were responsible for going from house to house to try to assess the degree of need in a household and family.[27]

The parochial records of Eton College do not indicate that Sumner took much part in the occasional offices at Eton College Chapel.[28] The only baptisms he performed there were those of his own children and there is record of his officiating at only one wedding and that was in 1818. It seems to have been the case that Sumner spent most of his time preaching and ministering at the small Chapel of ease which had been erected in 1769 for the needs of the local tradespeople and poorer parishioners who were being crowded out of the College Chapel. Eton Chapel of Ease evidently attracted very good congregations during the years of Sumner's ministry because by 1819 the building was unable to accommodate all those who wished to attend the services. The College Fellows therefore undertook to rebuild the Chapel on a much larger scale. The new building was opened for worship in the autumn of 1820. Sumner who had evidently taken a leading part in the life and ministry of the old Chapel was invited back from Mapledurham rectory to preach the dedication Sermon on 29 October. The *Windsor and Eton Express* gave the following account of the occasion.

> On Saturday last the new Chapel at Eton, which has been erected for the accommodation of the inhabitants by the liberality of the Provost and Fellows of Eton College was opened for Divine Service. An admirably appropriate Sermon was preached by the Revd J.B. Sumner. The Chapel is a very neat building, particularly the interior, which is fitted up with great elegance. A most tasteful altar-piece has been presented to their native town, by Mr Ingalton and Mr Evans, artists of Eton, which in design and execution is highly creditable to their talent. We understand a subscription has been raised by the inhabitants for the purpose of making their grateful sense of the obligation to the College of Eton, by furnishing the Chapel with some handsome communion plate.
>
> Sumner's sermon which he entitled *The Christian's Encouragement to Prayer* was printed and sold by E. Williams. The discourse was based on Jesus' words in John Chapter 16 verse 23: 'Verily, verily, I say unto you, whatsoever ye shall ask the Father in my name, He will give it to you.' Sumner began by stressing the assurance we have that God hears our prayers and went on to dwell on the confidence which we have in praying because Christ is our mediator.

'My Brethren what a comfort, what a confidence is this.... He that was in the beginning with God, and is God, cares for you, watches over you, intercedes for you, and promises you whatever you ask the Father in his name, believing, you shall receive.'[29]

He concluded by urging all those present 'who love the ordinances of God' not to pray 'as a mere form'.[30] We must learn to feel our need of prayer and to pray from the heart.[31]

In these years at Eton Sumner took great delight in his family circle, visiting his mother at Milford and his brother Charles who was by this time curate of Highclere in Hampshire. He seems to have been particularly close to Charles and his wife, Jenny, and there was a frequent exchange of letters between them on a wide range of domestic and family matters. The two brothers appear to have taken a keen interest in each other's work and career prospects.

As these early years passed by, John Bird began to give himself increasingly to study and academic writing. Charles' wife was evidently impressed by his erudition and wrote in her journal after a visit to his Eton household: '*En Verité plus je le vois le plus je l'aime. Il est si bon. On devient sage en l'écoutant.*'[32] John's sister wrote more candidly of him: 'He has just the proportion of feeling which is sufficient for all practical purposes, yet I think his habits are too philosophical for him ever to be distinguished for usefulness.'[33] Maria's comment was perhaps proof that those who stand closest are not always in a position to make the most accurate assessments of peoples' capabilities. In the event John Bird proved to be a singularly practical and useful writer whose works were very widely valued and read. What is more, within ten years he was to become perhaps the most practical and in-touch bishop on the bench. Yet in the war years of the second decade of the nineteenth century who could have foreseen what was to come?

Two of Sumner's most significant published works belong to the Eton period of his life, *Apostolic Preaching considered in an Examination of St Paul's Epistles* (1815) and *A Treatise on the Records of the Creation and the Moral Attributes of the Creator* (1816). Both these works won immediate acclaim and went through numerous reprintings. *Apostolic Preaching*, whose section on the sacrament of initiation persuaded both Newman and Gladstone in favour of baptismal regeneration, went through nine editions. *A Treatise on the Records of the Creation*, which was a two-volume work, had seven editions.

Sumner began the first of these two works by assuring his readers that his one desire had been to set before his brethren in the ministry for their practical use, the example of the Apostles as preachers of the Gospel. It was, he stated, his aim 'to consider' the doctrines they insist upon, and their mode of enforcing them, so as to tend eventually to the greater edification of a single congregation'.[34] Sumner considered Paul's epistles as the fit model of instruction for the modern preacher because they were 'written to those who had already become Christians, and in general, dwell upon the topics of improvement and proficiency, instead of the doctrines of repentance and conversion.' However, Sumner is quick to point out that the supreme task of the Christian minister is an evangelistic one.

> Cases indeed may occur in which it may rather be a minister's business to convert, than to enlighten and improve: where he is called upon to take the part of a missionary, and to declare a revelation, instead of that of a guide.... To those, for instance, who with the name of Christians, have hitherto passed their lives without any religion whatever, the doctrine of conversion must be preached plainly and directly.[35]

The main body of the book is taken up with a detailed consideration of the great doctrines of the Christian faith, Predestination and Election, the corruption of Human Nature, Grace and Justification and Sanctification. In the matter of Predestination, Sumner is respectful of Calvin's learning, but averse to his system. Sumner did 'not desire to argue against predestination as believed in the closet, but as taught from the pulpit'.[36] In other words the doctrine may be of private consolation and encouragement but not appropriate in terms of sermon content. Nevertheless Sumner strongly opposed the doctrine of absolute decrees. 'What feelings of confidence can a congregation have,' he asked, 'which has been accustomed to hear, that a decree has gone out from God by which the final destiny of every man is irrevocably doomed?'[37] Sumner considered the teaching of Paul's letter to the Romans to be an explanation of God's conduct to the Jews and not therefore a basis by which to justify the general doctrine of decrees.[38]

In his discussion of human nature Sumner was emphatic that it is totally corrupt. 'Man', he asserted, 'is born with a corrupt heart, prone to sin, averse from holiness, and unable of himself to please God.'[39] This teaching must in Sumner's view never be lost sight of by the preacher.

> To relinquish this, is to relinquish the strongest hold possessed by the preacher over the feelings and consciences of his hearers. It is to give up a truth which is declared by the world without, and receives a concurrent testimony from the experience of the heart within.[40]

The chapter entitled 'On the Corruption of Human Nature' admirably prepares the way for the succeeding chapters on Grace and Justification. In his discussion of grace Sumner appears to state a doctrine on Baptismal regeneration:

> ... on the authority of this example, and of the undeniable practice of the first ages of Christianity; our Church considers Baptism as conveying regeneration, instructing us to pray, before baptism, that the infant 'may be born again and made an heir of everlasting salvation' and to return thanks after baptism, 'that it hath pleased God to regenerate the infant with his Holy Spirit, and to receive him for his own child by adoption'.[41]

Sumner goes on to qualify this statement by pointing out that after baptism many 'live profane and unholy lives, and perish in their sins. In view of this, the preacher must lead his hearers to look for some new conversion.'[42] On the matter of justification Sumner is emphatic that all of Paul's epistles teach justification by faith alone. The basis on which this justification is grounded on 'Christ's blood alone'.[43] Faith, as he understands it, implies 'a total reliance upon Christ in the whole work of our salvation—an entire renunciation of our own merits, considered as contributing towards it—a humble dependence that, "being justified by his blood", we shall also finally "be saved from wrath through him"'.[44]

Sumner concludes the volume with a section entitled 'On Intercourse with the World'. Here he gives a lengthy quotation from William Wilberforce's *Practical Christianity*, which makes the point that the Christian's strength is the temperate use of all the gifts and resources of the Creator.[45]

The evangelical *Christian Observer* in reviewing Sumner's volume felt duty-bound 'to suggest our doubts as to the soundness of some of his interpretations.'[46] Nevertheless it concluded on a most positive note considering 'the merits of this treatise as very far outweighing its imperfections.'[47] *A Treatise on the Records of Creation*, which was published by Hatchard in 1816, had been submitted the previous year for the Burnett essay competition and was awarded the second prize of £400 by the three assessors appointed by the members of Kings' and Marischal Colleges, Aberdeen.[48] The full title of Sumner's work was *A Treatise on the Records of the Creation and the Moral Attributes of the Creator with Particular Reference to Jewish History and to the Consistency of the Principle of Population.* In it Sumner advances two major arguments: first that the Mosaic Record of Creation is unique and second that the creation ordinances show the deity to be both wise and good. The first volume commences by establishing the proposition that something must have existed from eternity and that it is absurd to suppose that something to have been the material world. Sumner gives a fairly extensive discussion of the teleological argument and maintains that the instances of design with which the Universe abounds can only be ascribed to an intelligent creator: 'There we conclude, by a natural and irresistible analogy that a world which exhibits throughout an unbroken chain of contrivances and means... is the work, not of chance, but of an intelligent contriver.'[49]

Having established the unique origin of the creation, Sumner contends that some account of it would surely be revealed and preserved. Such indeed does exist 'professing to have been written by Moses, the leader and lawgiver of the Jews'.[50] Sumner dismisses the arguments of the early Church fathers that the Genesis account of the formation of the world must be seen as allegory.

> I would premise... that two unanswerable reasons must forbid us, however pressed with difficulties from resorting to the explanation.... My inquiry... supposes the Mosaic account to contain not allegory but fact.[51]

However Sumner did not feel it incumbent on him to press every last detail as historical fact.[52] He comments in an appendix at the end of Volume 1 that Moses' account of creation 'does not profess to furnish anything like systematic or elaborate detail of the mode in which the materials of the earth were brought to their actual form and situation'. Sumner summarised what in his view the Genesis account of the creation requires of us.

> First that God was the original Creator of all things: secondly, that at the formation of the globe... the whole of its materials were in a state of chaos and confusion: and thirdly, that at a period not exceeding five thousand years ago... the whole earth underwent a mighty catastrophe.[53]

At the time of Sumner's writing, geology was at a point where its findings did not substantially conflict with the Mosaic account of the origins of the universe. Sumner concluded: 'All I am concerned to establish, is the unreasonableness of supposing that geological discoveries as they have hitherto proceeded, are hostile to the Mosaic account of the creation.'[54] In the second and third Appendices Sumner went on to defend the Mosaic authorship of the Pentateuch and to assert the reasonableness of the human race having descended from a single pair.

It was the second volume of *A Treatise on the Records of Creation* which attracted more attention on account of its justifying a hierarchical class system and its baptising of Malthusian economic and social theories as acceptable Christian doctrine. Sumner's overriding aim was to demonstrate that the present world order affirmed 'that the creator is endued with infinite power, wisdom and goodness'. He stated it in strident form in the first chapter. 'I contend', he wrote, 'that the slightest outline of the constitution of the natural world conveys a proof of the most comprehensive wisdom.'[55] Somewhat strangely perhaps, Sumner made no attempt to draw a distinction between the wisdom of God which can be seen in the natural world and that which can be seen in human and social relationships. Nor did he contrast the original created order before the Fall with that which subsequently emerged. He therefore felt it necessary to defend and justify those civilised nations such as his own contemporary England of the early nineteenth century which 'admits and consists of a gradation of ranks and unequal conditions'.[56]

The basis of Sumner's argument was that inequality of rank is best for man. It is this which motivates and spurs human beings to industry and creativity. In a discussion of the Indians of Guiana, Sumner wrote that 'living under the most perfect equality, they are not impelled to industry by that Spirit of emulation, which in Society leads to great and unwearied toil'.[57] The fact of the matter, as he saw it, was that men and women need 'an urgent stimulus to manual exertion.' An important aspect of this motivation is 'hope of improving fortune, and of accumulating property'.[58] At this point Sumner was merely rehearsing the contentions of the Scottish economist, Adam Smith, who had argued that a person would only labour if individual satisfaction was adequate.

In Chapter four Sumner makes the same point in more detail. 'The truth is' he wrote, 'the inequality' of conditions, which is the foundation of civil Society, affords not only the best improvement of human faculties, but the best trial of human virtues; it is the nursery most suited to their formation, and the theatre most suited to their 'exercise'.[59] The problem with Sumner's scheme, as later churchmen such as the Christian Socialists were to observe, was that it 'legitimised' the condition of poverty—indeed it regarded the poor as a God-ordained class. Sumner was not unaware of the implications of his theory which blatantly substantiated Marx's accusation that the Christian religion was an 'opiate' which kept the working-classes from a real awareness of the injustice of their condition.

It is perhaps true that the first prospect of a country far advanced in civilisation, appals us by the vast disproportion observable between the wealth of the few, and the poverty of many.... If mankind had no ulterior destination, and their enjoyment on earth was the sole end and purpose of their being, this dispro-portion would... be... inexplicable.[60]

It seems strange that a man of biblical convictions such as John Sumner could have contemplated such an idealised future ex-istence beyond the grave for the largely unchurched classes. Many of Sumner's evangelical contemporaries were consider-ably less optimistic about the matter. Sumner also went on to write forcibly that the social injustice of the situation made 'the exercise of judicious charity still more imperative'. Indeed it 'demands of the affluent not only a denial of some luxurious vanities, but what is often more reluctantly sacrificed, a portion of their time, and a sound exertion of discriminating judge-ment'.[61] In this demand for benevolence Sumner appeared to be unaware of the way in which charity kept the poor in a state of continued dependency and prevented them in engaging in self-help and so regaining a sense of dignity and self-worth.

Leaving aside the possibility of any consolation in a world to come, Sumner maintained that the poor could nevertheless find a degree of contentment in their present lot. Doubtless this was more possible for the farm workers who toiled in the pleasant meadowland and pastures surrounding Eton College than it was for the town labourers of the industrial north whose 'vale of tears' Sumner was not to contemplate at first hand for another decade.

It should perhaps be noted that Sumner drew a distinction between 'poverty' and 'indigence', that is poverty of an extreme form which cannot be part of a wise creator's pattern and is most usually self-inflicted by laziness or intemperate behav-iour. Sumner points up the contrast in the following passage:

> These conditions, it must ever be remembered, are essentially distinct and separate. Poverty is often both honourable and comfortable; but indigence can only be pitiable, and is usually contemptible. Poverty is not only the natural lot of many, in a well-constituted society, but is necessary that a society may be well-constituted.

In contrast to poverty Sumner saw indigence as reprehensible. It can be avoided given proper motivation and adequate human effort.

> Indigence, on the contrary, is seldom the natural lot of many, but is commonly the state into which intemperance and want of prudent foresight push poverty: the punishment which the moral government of God inflicts in this world upon thoughtlessness and guilty extravagance.[62]

Sumner suggested a variety of devices for avoiding indigence including the postponement of marriage[63] on the part of the lower orders of society. Indigence clearly could not be seen as established by a wise creator. This led Sumner on to assert that the creator had established a principle of population control which 'will keep a society of various ranks and conditions in a constant state of balance'.[64] Populations will tend to multiply up to the level of food supply and remain fairly static at that point. Indigence will not therefore feature in well-balanced civilised societies. When a population level reaches a maximum for the available food supply the resultant pressure will either result in migrations or famine conditions and then ill health and subsequent increases in the death rate.

What Sumner had in fact done was to take Malthus' theories that poverty, for all except the fortunate few, is inevitable and that redistribution is powerless to effect any lasting change, and to give them a specifically biblical and Christian frame of reference. Thus whereas Malthus argued for example that institutions such as law, private property and marriage were the natural result of the competitive struggle in an overpopulated world, Sumner maintained they were actually purposed and planned by the all-wise Judeo-Christian deity. Sumner's *Treatise* was a significant work in that it came to affect the social thinking of subsequent generations of Victorian Churchmen of all persuasions. It gave them a clear mandate for the view expressed by Mrs Alexander's hymn of 1848 that:

> The rich man in his castle
> The poor man at his gate
> God made them high or lowly
> And ordered their estate.

A.M.C. Waterman has gone further, maintaining that by 1833 political economists had constructed a system on the main features of Sumner's thinking and produced an ideological system which was to dominate popular if not intellectual thinking to the end of the nineteenth century.[66] It showed itself in current thought such as *laissez-faire* economics and pleas for an open market free from import tariffs on food stuffs and new materials.

In many ways Sumner's thinking in the *Treatise* is decidedly in the spirit of the eighteenth century. As has been pointed out, despite his generally mainstream Anglican theology, he demonstrated a remarkably Calvinistic view of society and the social order. Later however, circumstances were to cause Sumner to be rather more restrained. At the end of the French wars, the returning soldiers created a glut of surplus labour, and this together with the Corn Laws which kept bread prices at an artificially high level led to starvation in some areas of the country. All this meant 'indigence' on a widespread scale. Thus in 1820s and 30s Sumner and his associates no longer spoke in optimistic tones of the ability of laws of economy to right the lot of the poor. Instead Sumner's theme was that set out in his first episcopal charge that the poor needed to be reconciled 'to hardships and privations, as the intended trial of his faith, the lot of many of God's most approved servants'. Sumner's only solution henceforward was that common to all Churchmen, namely that poverty and hardship were to be alleviated on a charitable basis with no criticism of the system which had produced such terrible conditions of hardship and poverty.

It is all too easy from a twentieth-century vantage point—a time in which we are conditioned from an early age to think in terms of equal opportunity—to dismiss Sumner's theories out of hand. However, in its time *A Treatise on the Records of Creation* was highly regarded and passed through seven editions. Following only a year after his *Apostolic Preaching*, it brought Sumner into the public eye as a thoughtful writer, and a scholar of some distinction. It came as no surprise therefore that in 1817 he was elected a Fellow of Eton College. This meant that he was now relieved of his teaching responsibilities in the school and possessed a substantial income which enabled him to devote more time to serious academic study and writing. His brother, Charles, and sister-in-law, Jenny, were, needless to say, delighted at this appointment. In a letter which Charles received from his friend S.T. Coleridge, the poet wrote:

> I congratulate you as *ab imo* on your brother's election—it is not half of what he deserves. The leisure which he has now for professional studies will, I trust, be beneficial to the Church. If he could devise some conciliatory mode of bringing good people together who are squabbling about words, what a blessing it would be.[67]

One of the very few personal possessions of John Bird to have survived, is a small notebook which relates to the latter months of 1817 following his appointment to the fellowship. One entry shows how very concerned he was that the time now entrusted to him should be used as a trust before God and not as leisure. The disciplined routine which Sumner set for himself was typical of the Simeonite evangelicals.

> Dressed by half past seven. Study to prayers. I study from ten to one. Exercise and dinner to half past five. Study two hours in the evening. Seven hours out of twenty four, which are arranged, is but little for intellectual employment; yet I do not forsee how it will be easy to average more; and even to this scheme many interruptions will invariably occur.[68]

Again on the same theme Sumner comments on the dangers attending the social round: 'Dinner visits can seldom be rendered really profitable to the mind. The company are so much occupied that little good is to be done.' Sumner comes back to his central concern that a minister must keep his sense of the value of time.[69]

A few months following his election as a Fellow, John renewed his acquaintance with Edinburgh, spending the Christmas season in the city, in all probability with the Robertsons.[70] In a letter penned to his brother Charles on 31 December he wrote:

> ... this is a wonderful city. I was surprised to find I could be so much surprised at renewing my acquaintance with the 'romantic

town.' Such indeed it is—houses, castle, spires, towers, hills, rocks, all rising one above another, and presenting an infinite variety of charms. Though it is winter, the outlines are grand and impressive, so much so as to lose little of their beauty. I must bring back some memoranda to make your curiosity eager, and I do not believe the world, take it all in all, has such another city.[71]

Notes

1. See *Times* (London) 8 September 1862. Sumner's obituary gives details of his commencing work at Eton.
2. Sumner's ordination papers, Wiltshire County Archives MS D1/14/1/25.
3. Sumner's subscription to the Thirty-Nine Articles, Wiltshire County Archives, MS D1/22/15.
4. See Bishop's Register, Wiltshire County Archives, MS D1/2/29.
5. See *Crockford's Clerical Directory*, 1860.
6. See *Dictionary of National Biography* Vol. XVI p. 1305, entry for Thomas Campbell Robertson.
7. *Kenilworth Baptismal Register*, Warwick County Record Office, MS DR/101/5.
8. See *Dictionary of National Biography*.
9. Marriage Register, St. Mary Walcot, Somerset Record Office, 31 March 1803.
10. See Venn, *Alumni Cantabrigienses* entry for 'Robertson, Love'.
11. Baptismal Register Eton College, Bucks County Record Office MS PR/72/1/14Q.
12. Maxwell Lyte H.C., *A History of Eton College 1440–1910* (Macmillan & Co., 1911), p. 388.
13. Anon, *Memoir of the Rev. F. Hodgson* Vol ii, p. 109.
14. Maxwell Lyte, H.C., *op. cit.*, p. 390.
15. *Ibid.*
16. *Ibid.*
17. Wilkinson C.A., *Reminiscences of Eton* (London, Hurst & Blackett Ltd., 1888), p. 117.
18. Wilkinson C.A., *ibid.* p. 118

19. Anon, *Etoniana Ancient and Modern Being Notes of the History and Traditions of Eton College* (William Blackwood & Sons, Edinburgh, 1865), p. 97.

20. *Ibid.*, p. 103.

21. Maxwell Lyte H.C., *op. cit.*, pp. 374–375.

22. Sterry W., *Annals of King's College and of our Lady of Eton Beside Windsor* (London, Methuen, 1908).

23. See Benson A.C., *Fasti Etonienses A Biographical History of Eton* (London, Simpkin, Marshall & Co., 1899), p. 273. This nickname is also substantiated by Cust L., *A History of Eton College* (London, Duckworth, 1899), p. 169.

24. Benson A.C. *op. cit.*, p. 273.

25. Liddon H.P., *Life of Edward Bouverie Pusey* (London, Hyman) Vol. I, p. 17.

26. Carus W., *Memoirs of the Life of the Rev Charles Simeon* (London, J. Hatchard & Son, 1848), pp. 64–65.

27. Moule H.C.G., *Charles Simeon* (London, IVP, 1956), p. 49.

28. See Marriage and Baptismal registers, Bucks. County Record Office.

29. *The Windsor and Eton Express*, 5 November 1820.

30. Sumner J.B., *The Christian's Encouragement to Prayer A Sermon Preached October 29th 1820, By the Revd. J.B. Sumner Fellow of Eton College & Co.* (printed and sold by E. Williams), British Museum MS 4476 h. 84, p. 12.

31. *Ibid.* p. 12.

32. Sumner G.H., *Life of Charles Richard Sumner DD Bishop of Winchester* (John Murray, 1876), p. 41.

33. Benson A.C., *Benson A.C.*, *op. cit.*, p. 273.

34. Sumner, J.B. *Apostolic Preaching Considered* (eighth edition, London, Hatchard & Son, 1839) p.v.

35. *Ibid.*, p. 29.

36. *Ibid.*, p. 40.

37. *Ibid.*, p. 72.

38. *Ibid.*, p. 55.

39. *Ibid.*, p. 117.

40. *Ibid.*, p. 118.

41. *Ibid.*, p. 160.

42. *Ibid.*, p. 160.

43. *Ibid.*, p. 207.
44. *Ibid.*, p. 209.
45. *Ibid.*, p. 298.
46. *Christian Observer*, 1815 p. 327.
47. *Ibid.*, p. 327.
48. See *Gentleman's Magazine*, 1815 Vol. LXXV, Pt.2, p.155 for full details.
49. Sumner J.B., *A Treatise on the Records of Creation*, 2 volumes (London, Hatchard, 1816), Vol. I p. 26.
50. *Ibid.*, Vol. I, pp. 30–31.
51. *Ibid.*, Vol. I, pp. 39–40.
52. *Ibid.*, Vol. I, pp. 269–270.
53. *Ibid.*, Vol. I, p. 272.
54. *Ibid.*, Vol. I, p. 283.
55. *Ibid.*, Vol. I, p. 272.
56. *Ibid.*, Vol. I, p. 283.
57. *Ibid.*, Vol. 2, p. 12.
58. *Ibid.*, Vol. 2, p. 44.
59. *Ibid.*, Vol. 2, p. 44.
60. *Ibid.*, Vol. 2, p. 76.
61. *Ibid.*, Vol. 2, p. 85.
62. *Ibid.*, Vol. 2, p. 86.
63. *Ibid.*, Vol. 2, p. 92.
64. *Ibid.*, Vol. 2, p. 317.
65. *Ibid.*, Vol. 2, p. 102.
66. Waterman A.M.C., 'The Ideological Alliance of Political Economy and Christian Theology 1798–1833', *Journal of Ecclesiastical History* Vol. 34, April 1983, p. 242.
67. Sumner G.H., *op. cit.*, p. 38. The 'leisure' referred to was because the fellows of Eton College were not required to teach in the School. They were paid to engage in research.
68. Sumner J.B., *Personal Notebook 1817* (Cumbria County Record Office), p. 14.
69. *Ibid.*, p. 12.
70. *Ibid.*, p. 12.
71. Sumner G.H., *op. cit.*, pp. 39–40.

3

Mapledurham Vicarage

John Bird's writing soon brought him a degree of fame and in recognition of his abilities the valuable college living of Mapledurham was offered to him in the summer of 1818. Mapledurham was a pleasant village of some 520 souls situated on the banks of the Thames not far from Reading. Eton College had possessed the patronage of the Church since the time their institution was founded in 1441. The income stood at £735 and in addition there were 47½ acres of glebe land. The *Record* Newspaper stated that Sumner's income from the parish was of the order of £1,000 per annum.[1] In addition Sumner's College fellowship yielded him an extra £800 per annum. He was therefore by the standards of his day a wealthy man.

The parish had a substantial parsonage house and Sumner and his family resided in it for the greater part of the year. Later when Sumner was elected to a Canonry of Durham Cathedral[2] he was required to be in residence in the city for three months annually. The parish's chief landowners were the Blount family who resided at Mapledurham House within the village community. They were Roman Catholics and had their own chapel attached to their house which was served by a resident priest.[3] The only other religious influence in the village was, according to Sumner, supplied by 'various teachers of different sects (who) attend in a room on Sunday afternoon, chiefly from Reading. They have a School for such children as will attend and service afterwards.'[4] In a report to the diocesan authorities Sumner gave the number of Dissenters as five families besides the papists. The greater part of the population were agricultural labourers and their families who lived in small cottages 'at the distance of from 1 to 2 miles from the Church, but no part further'.[5]

John Bird was admitted and instituted to the living on the 20 November 1818, by the Bishop of Oxford, Edward Legg.[6] Sumner succeeded J. Edward Chew who died whilst in office. There was a curate, Robert Baker, who resided nearby at Goring Heath, although he appears to have left the parish later the following year. Sumner was presented to the bishop by John Goodhall, the first Headmaster under whom he had worked, and who was now Provost of the College.

As one would expect from a man of Sumner's disposition and conscientious habits he was a model country clergyman. He held services every Sunday in the mornings at eleven and in the afternoon at three from Michaelmas to Lady Day and half-past-four in the summer.[7] Typically Sumner celebrated the sacrament three or four times a year, reporting in 1820 an average of 30 to 40 communicants.[8] Significantly three years later Sumner reported 'about 50 communicants' at each celebration.[9] This, though an increase on previous levels of attendance, was still below 10% of the population.

John Bird was a resident parson reporting in 1820: 'I reside in the parsonage house and serve my own cure during 8 months of the year. Mr.Brentford, resident at Caversham, assists me in my absence and is as near to the greater part of the population as the parsonage.'[10] A brief survey of the parish registers shows that Sumner took the occasional offices seriously and officiated at more than three-quarters of all the baptisms and at the majority of the marriages.[11] Sumner's parish was clearly a delight to him in many respects. He enjoyed his residence and wrote in a letter that 'our retreat has really been delightful; our shrubs and trees and little improvements beginning to show themselves, and recompense the pains they have cost'. The work among his congregation also gave cause for encouragement and he remarked that he had 'derived more satisfaction than usual in my flock; and have reason to hope that there are some few names in Sardis inscribed in the book of God.'[12]

It was inevitable that a man of Sumner's ability would soon be recognised. In 1820 Shute Barrington (1734–1826) who was very favourably impressed by Sumner's writings collated him to a stall in his Cathedral.[13] He wrote of his great happiness to his brother.

My dear Charles,
I am going to surprise you with my unexpected news, happily of a pleasant nature. I have had a letter from the Bishop of Durham, acquainting me that a stall in his Church is on the point of becoming vacant and that he has no hesitation in offering it to me as the author of & Co., & Co.... You will anticipate my answer. Of course I will vacate my fellowship, I suppose at the end of the year.[14]

In a subsequent paragraph Sumner showed his natural modesty as well as his sense of accountability. 'I may truly say', he wrote 'that nothing could have been more unexpected to me than this advancement.... I cannot, or ought not to feel but that my great prosperity imposes on me a most alarming responsibility'. Sumner duly resigned his fellowship and gave himself wholly to the work of his parish and his Cathedral responsibilities. The archives of the Dean and Chapter of Durham show that Sumner regularly put in the ten weeks a year ordinary residence in Durham required of a Canon, and attended Chapter meetings while there, but otherwise seems to have made no particular impression on the life of the Cathedral.[15] Interestingly Sumner retained his Cathedral stall until 1848. Presumably he resigned it on his appointment to Canterbury. Nevertheless he was strictly speaking a pluralist for the whole of his Chester episcopate.[16]

Writing

Mapledurham being a small parish gave Sumner ample time to continue with his writing projects. He was also in demand as a preacher at a variety of public occasions. With the passing of the years and his opportunity to converse with the poor in his own parish, Sumner's views began to mellow in response to the practical realities of everyday living.

In 1821 Sumner published *A Series of Sermons on the Christian Faith and Character*. This lengthy volume was dedicated to his recent patron 'the Venerable Bishop of Durham'.[17] A number of the addresses were prepared for and addressed to the scholars at Eton. Sumner clearly aimed to teach the principles of Christianity and to show how those principles influence the heart and conduct. Taken as a whole the sermons tend to lay stress on the ethical aspects of Christianity rather than on communion with God. Some of Sumner's evangelical reviewers felt that there was not enough stress on personal religion.[18] It was nevertheless a popular volume which ran to seven editions by 1824.[19]

In the same year Sumner produced *The Evidence of Christianity derived from its Nature and Reception*.[20] In this extensive work Sumner set out to defend Christianity on the basis of the internal evidence. He considered such issues as the proofs of Jesus' existence, the ring of truth in Christianity which stems from its systematic opposition to prevailing first-century Jewish opinion and the fulfilment of prophecies concerning the destruction of Jerusalem.[21]

When it came to considering economic and social issues, Sumner's views were much tempered when compared to the opinions he ventured in his 1815 *Treatise on the Records of Creation*[22] and his article on the Poor Laws in the *British Review* for 1817.[22] There his conviction was that the nation was capable of sustaining an expanding population and creating a sufficiency of job opportunities to enable the well-motivated to live in relative comfort.

In the *Evidence of Christianity* Sumner's earlier confidence was spiritualised away. Life for most people would continue 'inevitably poor and laborious', perpetuated from generation to generation. Only the gentle beauties of faith could provide relief and dignity to 'the lowest stations and meanest pursuits'.[23]

In 1828 Sumner's writing returned to a more specifically pastoral emphasis when he published *Four Sermons on Subjects relating to the Christian Ministry*.[24] Taken together the sermons epitomise the convictions of a Simeonite evangelical incumbent. In the first sermon, which was preached at an ordination held by his brother Charles at Farnham Castle, John Bird urged the candidates not to treat anyone as 'a subject of Christ, who knows of Christ nothing but the name.'[25] In the second sermon, entitled 'Encouragements and discouragements of the Christian Minister', Sumner urged on his hearers the supreme joy of seeing people come to faith in Christ. 'What', he asked 'ought to be the feeling of the Christian Minister when he is made the agent of the conversion of a sinner from darkness to light?' His reply was 'happiness which is even felt in heaven, where is fullness of joy and pleasures for evermore'.[26] The other two sermons on 'The superintendence of Christ over his Church', and 'The importance of the Ministerial Office' are equally characterised by the same gracious but godly seriousness which was so prevalent in early nineteenth-century evangelical religion in the established Church. Yet for all this Sumner was no obscurantist. In the very same year as the publication of his sermons, The *Christian Observer* noted that his views on Genesis had been condemned in a recent publication entitled *Scriptural Geology*. Sumner had from an early point parted company with the view that the Genesis account of the creation was not a scientific one. He was therefore put down as one of those who 'admit the Bible is not infallible'.[27] The *Christian Observer* however defended Sumner, maintaining that 'the well-informed part of the Christian public' would not regard the likes of Sumner as the 'allies of infidelity' solely for the reason that they maintain that 'there is nothing in revelation, justly interpreted, which is inconsistent with geological phenomena'.[28]

The Poor Law Question

Throughout his incumbency at Mapledurham Sumner continued to think and write about the Poor Law and the effect it had on society. At the end of the Napoleonic wars, with the return of demobilised soldiers the expense of the poor law supplement reached the staggeringly large total of £5,072,028.[29] This sum was nearly three times the amount paid out in relief immediately before the war. The result of this increasing commitment was that both clergy and laity began to question whether this system of institutional relief was the best way to fulfil their obligations. In 1818–19 in an effort to stem the rising cost of relief, Parliament legislated that able-bodied poor must prove they were unemployed for reasons outside their control.[30]

In earlier years Sumner displayed a certain reluctance to change the existing arrangements. He saw clearly that they supplemented the low pay of hard-working labourers to make up an adequate wage. However he came to believe that the problem was really a moral one. He was troubled that the Poor Law pay-outs discouraged individual responsibility on the part of the work-force. They had little or no motivation to look for work particularly in the cold wet winter season if relief was readily at hand.

In the immediate post-war years many clergy were persuaded by Malthus that the common people would have been much happier if the Poor Laws had never existed. Perhaps as a result of rubbing shoulders with farm labourers in his own parish on a daily basis, Sumner began to follow suit. In articles written during his Mapledurham years for the *Edinburgh Review* and the *Encyclopaedia Britannica* in 1822 and 1824,[31] Sumner became increasingly hostile to the system as it was then constituted. The article which he was invited to submit to the *Edinburgh Review* was never published, but the letters which he wrote to the editor, Macvey Napier, reveal some of the factors that had had an impact on Sumner's thinking. In accepting the invitation to produce the article Sumner wrote that the Poor Laws had 'at different times been strongly forced upon my attention, which must be the case in England with anyone who resides in the country and thinks about the condition of the labouring class'.[32] Later when submitting the article Sumner wrote:

> You will perceive that I am a decided enemy of the system; and in fact I become more so every day, from what I see of its effects. I believe indeed that now there are few of a different opinion in

theory: but to make any practical alteration will require a large portion of political courage.[33]

The Poor Law question subsided briefly in the mid 1820s, but with the 'Captain Swing' riots and agrarian disturbances of the early 1830s, matters came to a head once more. These disturbances were most severe in areas where allowances were paid and many therefore began to call for their abolition.[34] Early in 1832 the government appointed a Special Commission to study the question. Sumner was one of the two clerical commissioners. He joined the commission convinced that the Poor Law should be abolished.

Preaching and Society Meetings

When not writing or attending to his parochial duties, Sumner devoted a not inconsiderable portion of his time to preaching and attending meetings in connection with religious societies. There is no evidence that he was an outstanding or charismatic preacher, but he was clearly careful in his preparation and fluent in his style and delivery. At any event he was in demand as a preacher at a number of public occasions during his time as incumbent at Mapledurham. Among the significant addresses which Sumner gave were the Sermon at the Opening of the New Chapel of Ease at Eton in 1820, the Radcliffe Commemoration Sermon at Oxford in 1823, the Church Missionary Society Annual General Sermon at St Bride's, Fleet Street in 1825, the sermon at his brother's Consecration as Bishop of Llandaff in 1826, a sermon preached at the ordination held by his brother in January 1828 and, later the same year, the Graduation Sermon at Cambridge University in St Mary's Church. Many of these sermons were subsequently published and in some cases widely circulated. Sumner's sermon construction and technique is much after the style of Charles Simeon. He always begins with a text. This is then explained and the whole concluded with a challenge to some practical aspect of Christian living. In all his preaching John Bird's evangelicalism is clearly visible. In his sermon at the Annual General Meeting of the Church Missionary Society,[35] Sumner began with his text Matthew Chapter 10

verse 8: 'Freely ye have received. Freely Give.' He stated that
he had selected it because it contained the scriptural argument
for Missionary enterprise. After discussing the text in some
detail Sumner emphasised the sacrifice involved in becoming
an ambassador among the heathen'. The chief impediments as
he perceived them were 'parents and relations who... too often
extinguish feelings which burn with a desire to promote the
glory of God and the salvation of mankind'.[36] In his sermon at
Lambeth[37] on the occasion of his younger brother Charles'
consecration as Bishop of Llandaff he took as his text 1 Timo-
thy, Chapter 4 verse 16: 'Take heed unto thyself, and unto thy
doctrine; continue in them; for in doing this, thou shalt both
save thyself and them that hear thee.' The subject of his sermon
was the work of the Christian Missionary. In the first part
Sumner stressed in particular the importance of maintaining
apostolic doctrine. He then went on to underline the crucial
importance of looking on the world 'not with the cold indiffer-
ence of latitudinarian philosophy' but 'with a Christian's eye and
Christian's pity, as lying in darkness and the shadow of death.
He read its state in the sacrifice of the cross. If Christ died for
all, then all were dead'.[38]

At his brother's first ordination service at Farnham Castle on
Sunday 20 January 1828 Sumner spoke of the task of extending
Christ's Kingdom.[39] In elaborating the qualities necessary for
such a task John Bird displayed his evangelical convictions to
the full.

> Now nothing, except personal experience and careful observ-
> ance, would convince anyone how far a nominally Christian
> Kingdom is from being a really Christian Kingdom. I have no
> wish to narrow the entrance of heaven; but dare I make it wider
> than Scripture has represented? Can I call him a subject of
> Christ, who makes the Gospel no rule either of his sentiments
> or his practice? Whose desires are bounded, and whose actions
> are governed by the objects and principles of this world?[40]

Speaking at the Cambridge University Commencement Service
in June 1828[41] Sumner chose as his text Matthew, Chapter 3
verse 16 'The testimony of the Father to his beloved Son'. 'The
great business of religion' he said, was 'to bring the mind of

men into conformity with the mind of God'. Sumner was
making the point that just as God approved His Son so he
approves those whose minds are in conformity with his mind.
This is not an easy task for anyone. It needs constant vigilance.
Sumner exhorted his newly graduating congregation:

> Be not content with coldly subscribing to the fact of Christ's
> Cross and passion, as to an article of faith; but accustom your
> hearts to acknowledge the justice of God in condemning sin,
> and to feel his mercy in accepting those who approach him in
> 'the Beloved'.

Sumner went on to speak of learning in high tones declaring it
to be honourable and the means of reputation and advancement
in the world. 'But', he declared, 'it may do more: it may also
glorify God'.[42]

Aside from his preaching John Bird appears to have spent
other time out of his parish taking an active role in the work of
various societies both secular and religious. He seems to have
been much concerned with the plight of the Irish. In June 1822
the *Reading Mercury* published a list of those who had contributed money to a fund set up in the town to aid 'the wretched
condition of the peasantry in the town of Sligo'.[43] Sumner is
listed amongst the subscribers as having donated £5. The same
paper carried a lengthy report in July 1828 of the Anniversary
proceedings of the Berkshire Irish Association. Sumner who
was one of a number of local clergy who was present and took
part in the meeting. Sumner's interest in the Association may
well have been heightened by its concern to promote the British
and Foreign Bible Society's newly published Irish language
text of the Bible.[44] A little later in the early autumn Sumner was
present at the Tenth Anniversary of the Berkshire Church
Missionary Association and proposed several resolutions.[45]

Family Circle

The years at Mapledurham seem to have been a singularly
happy time for John Bird as he gave himself to the pastoral work
of his parish and continued to find time to write. Doubtless he
also enjoyed the regular stimulus of the Durham Cathedral

Chapter. One occasion of sadness was the unexpected death of
his younger brother Henry, who died whilst at sea on board his
own ship. John Bird wrote to his close friend Edward Hawke
Locker (1777–1849).

> I am sure you and Mrs. L. will sincerely sympathise with us in
> the loss of my brother who died after 2 days' fever on board his
> ship the Elphinstone.... Poor fellow—hardships and frequent
> dysentries had injured his constitution—and he was unable to
> withstand a fresh attack. My sincere trust is that he knew in
> whom he believed, and was living in the faith of his Saviour
> Since he had a ship of his own he had always conducted it in
> Xtian [sic] manner, with regular prayers and every attention to
> religious duty—and these are the things which the mind reverts
> to now and feels the value of.[46]

During this time Sumner's wife Marianne remained in good
health and it was during these years that his two sons, John
Henry and Robert George were born.[47] Another happy family
occasion was the marriage of his daughter Anne to the Revd.
James Colpoys at Mapledurham on 14 October 1828. His
brother Charles, recently consecrated Bishop of Winchester,
officiated at the ceremony.[48] Extant letters reveal a deep bond
of affection between John and his younger brother Charles. It
may well be that it was at Eton, when John was a tutor and his
younger brother a pupil, that their relationship moved from
being a conventional familial bond to something closer to an
alliance. Whilst John was at Mapledurham, Charles took up
residence at Highclere not far from Newbury which was within
easy travelling distance. It was their mutual delight to visit one
another's families and to enjoy regular communication.

John and his brother carried on a fairly voluminous correspondence which is well documented by G.H. Sumner's biography of his father Charles Sumner. Shortly after Charles and
Jenny had settled at Highclere, Charles was offered the position
of 'Master of an endowed school at Enniskillen. The position
seems to have come through the influence of the Claphamite,
Charles Grant.[49] Charles considered the matter carefully and
consulted John for further guidance. John Bird's letter to his

younger brother reveals an astute blend of practical advice and
worldly wisdom.

> Should you continue your present situation and plan, you may
> reasonably expect in the course of ten or fifteen years a living
> of £300 or £400 per annum for some quarter or other, and that
> probably would be the extent of your preferment.... If you take
> it, you cannot be wrong in following such a lead of Providence
> to a work of great importance and usefulness; if you decline you
> cannot be wrong in preferring... a sphere of greater noise and
> ambition.[50]

Having set out the two alternative courses John Bird concluded
by emphasising the fact that a decision which would influence
the whole of Charles' future life demanded 'a solemn entreaty
that you may be enlightened with wisdom from above, and
enabled to decide in the way that shall prove pleasing to God,
and most favourable to the great business of our present state
of living'.[51] It is interesting to reflect that John anticipated that
within ten years his brother might hope for a living with an
income of perhaps £300 or £400. Within a decade his brother
had been consecrated to the see of Winchester which was
considered to be worth £10,000 annually in 1836.[52]

There seems to have been no hint of jealousy or rivalry
between the brothers. When Charles who was ten year his
brother's junior was appointed to the bishopric of Llandaff in
March 1826, John wrote to him in terms of fulsome praise and
congratulation.

> This moment, five o'clock, Tuesday I open your letter for the
> first time.... Most heartily glad I am for your own sake, and for
> the Church's sake, that you are safely seated on the bench....
> You have so conducted yourself in every situation which you
> have yet filled that I feel a certain confidence for the future. You
> will be an instrument in promoting both the glory of God and
> the good of mankind. Marianne regrets that she cannot write
> herself this afternoon.... The girls are already pleasing them-
> selves with familiarising to themselves the phrase, My Uncle,
> the bishop? I will write further about Consecration sermon at
> an early opportunity.[53]

A day or so later John wrote again to his brother that he had
received 'a very kind letter from the Bishop of Gloucester
congratulating me on your advancement, and speaking of you
in the most handsome terms'. He also 'readily' consented to
preach.[54] Later in June, Charles reflected in a letter a friend:
'John's sermon at Lambeth yesterday week was, as I had
anticipated, an excellent one. The text was 1 Tim iv 16. It is to
be printed, and I shall send out a copy by the first opportunity.'[55]
To Edward Locker John Bird wrote: 'What a great event my
brother Charles' promotion is! and what a steady friend his
Majesty has been to him! He has so filled the other situations
in which he has been placed, that I trust he will fulfil the high
duties of a bishopric so that neither himself nor others shall have
reason to regret his appointment.'[56]

By the later 1820s John Bird was becoming widely known.
He was frequently present at the Annual Meetings of major
religious societies and preached a growing number of sermons
on public occasions. His writings continued to find publishers
and were read by increasing numbers of clergy and laity. His
work as a Prebend of Durham Cathedral brought him into
contact with many influential clergy and laity. Added to all of
this, his younger brother Charles had tutored the children of the
King's mistress, the Marchioness of Conyngham, and continued to have audiences with the King himself.[57] It was inevitable
that before very long John Bird would follow in his brother's
footsteps to find a place on the bench of bishops.

Charles had taken the opportunity to introduce his brother to
the King and to the Conynghams, but it is not clear whether
they were personally influential in securing his promotions as
some historians have argued. Baring-Gould, who was no friend
of the evangelicals, stated boldly that Charles was 'able to
introduce his brother John Bird to George IV and with the
continued favour of the Marchioness, obtained for him the
Bishopric of Chester.[58] Ford K. Brown takes the same view,[59]
although, as E.R. Moore has pointed out, there is no evidence
for this.[60] In the autumn of 1827 Sumner was offered the
bishopric of Sodor and Man.[61] After careful consideration he
declined the appointment only to be offered in August the

following year, the see of Chester.[62] The *Reading Mercury* commented warmly:

> We have much pleasure in announcing the elevation of Dr Summer... to the see of Chester.... Dr Sumner's appointment to the Prebend gave, we believe, unqualified satisfaction to every friend of high merit and of the Church of England; and we do not doubt that the further advancement with which he has now been honoured will be the source of equal gratification.[63]

Sumner's appointment was widely acclaimed. Charles Anderson of Oriel College wrote to Samuel Wilberforce: 'By the way we hail the second Sumner's elevation to Chester... The bench of bishops will soon be what it ought to be.'[64] John Henry Newman wrote to Keble: 'I have just heard of the appointment of John Sumner to Chester, which has given me sincere pleasure. I suppose it will be generally popular...'[65] Sumner was consecrated in September and moved to face the challenge of presiding over the most populous diocese in England.[66]

Notes

1. Gardener M.D., *Gazetteer and Dictionary of the County of Oxford* (Gardener, 1852), p. 724. This figure of £735 is for the year 1841. The *Record* 5 May 1862 stated that the total income for the living in Sumner's time was £1,000 p.a.
2. *Reading Mercury*, 30 October 1820.
3. See *Visitation Return*, 1820 (Ms Oxf. Diocese d. 579).
4. *Ibid.*, question 4.
5. *Ibid.*, question 1.
6. *Notebook of Bishop Edward Legg* (Oxford Diocesan Records) p. 38. Edward Legg was Bishop of Oxford (1815–27).
7. *Visitation Return* 1820, question 6.
8. *Ibid.*, question 7.
9. *Visitation Return* 1823, question 7.
10. *Ibid.*, question 10.
11. See *Mapledurham Baptismal Register* 1813–1867 MS DD (Oxford Diocesan Archives) and *Mapledurham Register of Marriages* 1813–37. For example in 1822 out of a total of twenty baptisms Sumner officiated at sixteen. In 1824 out of a total of seventeen

baptisms Sumner officiated at fifteen. In 1819 out of a total nine weddings Sumner officiated at five, and in 1824 out of a total of seven weddings Sumner officiated at five.

12. Sumner J.B. to Edward Locker 16 May 1821 (Locker Papers, Huntingdon Library, San Marino, California, USA).
13. Fowler M., *Some Notable Archbishops of Canterbury* (London, SPCK, 1895), p. 155.
14. Sumner G.R., *Life of Charles Richard Sumner* (John Murray, 1872), pp. 52–53.
15. *Reading Mercury* 30 October 1820.
16. See *DCD Inst. Bk.* 4 f 143 v. Sumner was installed to the Ninth Stall on 4 November 1820; promoted to the Fifth Stall 11 May 1826; promoted to the Second Stall 1827 which he retained until 1848. See also *DCD Inst. Bk.* 4 f. 136.
17. Sumner J.B., *Sermons on the Christian Faith and Character* (London, 1821).
18. See for example *Christian Observer*, July 1821.
19. Sanders F., *Historic Notes on the Bishops of Chester*, p. 121.
20. Sumner J.B., *The Evidence of Christianity derived from its Nature and Reception* (1824), p. 429.
21. See especially *ibid.*, Chapters 1–3.
22. Sumner J.B. 'Reports on the Poor Law', *British Review* Vol. X, 1817, pp. 350–384.
23. Sumner J.B., *Evidences of Christianity, Divorced from its Nature and Reception* (2nd edition, 1826), p. 404 f.
24. Sumner J.B., *Four Sermons on Subjects relating to the Christian Ministry* (London, 1828).
25. *Ibid.*
26. *Ibid.*
27. *Christian Observer*, Feb. 1828, p. 98.
28. *Ibid.*
29. Soloway R.A., *Prelates and People* (Routledge and Kegan Paul, 1969), p. 126.
30. *Ibid.*, p. 127.
31. *Ibid.*, p. 133.
32. *Napier Papers*, British Museum MSS 34,613 folio 12.
33. *Ibid.*, MSS 34,613, folio 53.
34. Woodward L., The Age of Reform (Clarendon, 1962), p. 450.

35. Sumner, J.B., *Sermon Preached at St. Bride's Church Fleet Street, on Monday Evening, May 2nd 1825 before the Church Missionary Society* (London, J. Hatchard & Son, 1826), pp. 1–28.
36. *Ibid.*, p. 22.
37. Sumner, J.B., *A Sermon preached at Lambeth May 21st 1826 at the Consecration of the Right Reverend Charles Richard Sumner Lord Bishop of Llandaff* (London, John Hatchard & Son, 1826).
38. *Ibid.*, p. 22.
39. Sumner J.B., *A Sermon Preached in the Chapel at Farnham Castle at an Ordination held by the Lord Bishop of Winchester on Sunday Jan 20th 1828* (Bodleian Library MS 28.534).
40. *Ibid.*, p. 6.
41. Sumner J.B., *A Sermon Preached at St. Mary's Church, Cambridge on Commencement Sunday 29th June 1828 and published by Command of His Royal Highness William Frederick, Duke of Gloucester, Chancellor of the University* (London, J. Hatchard & Son, 1828).
42. *Ibid.*, pp. 12, 15.
43. *Reading Mercury*, 3 June 1822.
44. *Ibid.*, 21 July 1828.
45. *Ibid.*, 8 September 1828.
46. Sumner J.B. to Edward Locker 21 January 1826.
47. John Henry Robertson Sumner (1821–1910) sometime Rector of Ellesborough, Buckingham, married Antoinette Maria Edwards (d. 1852) and later Elizabeth Ann Gibson. Robert George Moncrieff Sumner (1824–1885) became a barrister.
48. *Mapledurham Register of Marriages* 1813–37 (Oxford County Archives).
49. Sumner G.R., *op. cit.*, p. 51.
50. *Ibid.*, p. 50.
51. *Ibid.*, p. 50.
52. Winchester, See of, *A Dictionary of English Church History* (A.R. Mowbray & Co. Ltd., edn.), p. 665.
53. Sumner G.R., *Life of R.C. Sumner* (John Murray, 1872), pp. 101–102.
54. *Ibid.* p. 103. Sumner J.B. to Charles, 31 March 1826.
55. *Ibid.*, p. 112.
56. Sumner J.B. to Edward Locker, 29 March 1826.

57. See *ibid.*, p. 90.
58. Baring-Gould S., *The Evangelical Revival* (Methuen, 1920), p. 265.
59. Brown F.K., *Fathers of the Victorians* (Cambridge University Press, 1961), p. 62.
60. Moore E.R., *John Bird Sumner Bishop of Chester 1828–48* (unpublished MA thesis, University of Manchester, 1976), p. 21.
61. *Reading Mercury*, 29 October 1827.
62. *Ibid.*, 5 November 1827.
63. *Ibid.*, 4 August 1828. See also *Record*, 1 August 1828.
64. Wilberforce S., *Episcopal and Diocesan Papers*, Bodleian Library MS C189, cited by Moore E.R., *op. cit.*, p. 35.
65. Mozley A., *Letters and Correspondence of John Henry Newman*, 2 vols. (Longman Green & Co., 1891), Vol. 1, p. 189.
66. *Christian Observer*, October 1862.

4

Bishop of Chester

Early in 1828 Charles Blomfield was translated from Chester to London after only four years in office. Sumner was appointed his successor.

Sumner wrote a letter of acceptance from Eton College to the Duke of Wellington on 30 July. He expressed his 'sincere gratitude' for the King's 'high favour' and pledged his total commitment to 'the arduous situation to which his majesty has called me'.[1] Sumner was elected on the 3 September by the Dean and Chapter,[2] and Royal Assent was received two days later. He was consecrated at York on 14 September. The Archbishop was assisted by Sumner's brother, and the Bishops of Winchester and Gloucester. The Sermon was preached by the Revd. Thomas Gisborne (1758–1846), Squire of Yoxall Lodge.[3] Gisborne who was an intimate friend of William Wilberforce and an associate of the Clapham sect was a fellow Prebendary with Sumner at Durham Cathedral.

The Diocese

The Diocese of Chester was founded in 1541 and comprised the whole of Lancashire, Cheshire and Westmorland,[4] with parts of Cumberland and Yorkshire to the north, and parts of Flintshire and Denbighshire to the South. The river Ribble divided the diocese into the two archdeaconries of Chester and Richmond. This was an enormous geographical area which R.C. Richardson described as 'a poorly endowed, monstrously large and unmanageable unit'.[5]

Within the diocese the major concentration of population lay in the county of Lancashire which in 1831 had a total of 1,336,854 inhabitants.[6] Cumberland, Westmorland and North Lancashire which were scattered rural farming parishes presented an altogether different challenge. Cheshire was noted for cheese and salt whilst the southern part of Lancashire was to grow rapidly as a centre of industry with the development of the cotton mills. The heartland of this expansion was the town of Manchester with its surrounding settlements including the bustling and overcrowded port of Liverpool. Morris points out that in Manchester the population increased from 737,340 in 1821 to 1,605,919 in 1851.[7] Much of this was due to the fall in the death rate but also to successive nineteenth-century waves of immigration from Ireland.[8] This large concentration of Catholics may well have influenced Sumner to vote in favour of the Catholics in the Roman Catholic Emancipation Bill of 1829.[9]

Rapid population growth was to be one of the central features of the diocese during the time of Sumner's episcopate. Many of the inhabitants lived in appalling and squalid conditions. Sumner himself noted that in Liverpool 'one seventh of the whole population... live in cellar dwellings'. Similarly in Manchester and Salford 'out of one-hundred-and-eighty thousand persons of working-class, eighteen thousand live in cellars'. The cellar accommodations were often contaminated by piles of sewage and excrement of every kind, which were in places 20 feet high and 200 yards long. In Bury he observed that 'in a thousand and fifty houses, of which census was taken, the provision of beds was found to average only one in four of the population inhabiting them'.[10]

The Diocese of Chester was gradually slimmed down during the middle years of the nineteenth century. In 1847 and 1880 the new dioceses of Manchester and Liverpool were carved out of its territory. In addition parts of it were also transferred to the dioceses of Ripon (1836), St Asaph (1849) and Carlisle, including the whole of the county of Westmorland (1847) and parts of Cumberland (1856). Sumner who remained in office until 1848, continued to grapple with a very large territory with a burgeoning population for almost all of his episcopate.

There was an old saying that 'the Bishop of Chester never dies' which probably related to the fact that the income was low and the bishops moved on to better-salaried sees. Sumner's immediate predecessors George Law (1812–24) and Charles Blomfield (1824–28) were both able and conscientious men who laid the foundations for many of the reforms Sumner was to pursue. As a consequence of their efforts Sumner was able to write: 'I feel myself happy in succeeding to a road so admirably smoothed and prepared'.[11] The new bishop could also take encouragement from the fact that the number of pluralist and absentee clergy in the diocese was relatively small.[12]

Nevertheless a huge amount of work needed to be done in order to improve the low spiritual condition of all sections of the diocese. Four years later in his second charge to the clergy of the diocese, Sumner lamented the lack of attention being paid to basic Christian duties. He commented:

> We perceive, no less, the absence of other habits [viz]. The partial observance of the Sabbath: the rarity of domestic worship: the neglect of the Holy Table: the indifference of the young towards Scriptual instruction, the indifference of parents to the conduct of children...[13]

Sumner returned to this theme later in the same charge and lamented the almost total absence of family prayers,[14] and the lamentable ignorance of even the most basic tenets of the Christian faith. He cited one Lancaster family known to the parish visitor.

> One of them did not know there was any future state. She had heard of heaven and hell but did not understand the meaning of the words. And though both had heard the name Jesus Christ, that was all they knew about him. They did not know who made the world, nor had they ever heard of our first parents, or their fall.[15]

Among the large towns of the diocese, Manchester[16] appeared to be in a particularly poor state. It is worth noting that despite its population of some of 200,000 inhabitants, this seething

mass of people was still one parish with one parish church in
Sumner's time.[17]

Sumner's Strategy for the Diocese

Confronted by this immensely demanding and challenging
situation, Sumner soon demonstrated that he was very much
more than just a quiet scholar and country parson fitted only for
the gentlemanly pursuits of the Berkshire countryside. Within
a short period he began to transform the life and worship of the
entire diocese.

Sumner's plan had four key aspects: the greater provision of
Church accommodation, especially for the poor; the encouragement and support of the clergy; the advocacy of lay visitors and
lay-helpers; and the promotion of education.

Church-building

Sumner soon recognised what Horace Mann's 1851 Census of
religion was later to show, namely that many working men and
women in the diocese were prevented from going to church not
by their own inclinations, but by the shortage of churches for
them to go to. This problem was particularly acute in the
populous districts of Manchester, Liverpool, Preston and Blackburn. Sumner immediately set about encouraging the building
of new places of worship. Some 49 new church buildings were
erected in the first four years of his episcopate.[18] Despite this
significant achievement Sumner lamented in his charge of 1832
that the county of Lancashire was 'still grievously in want of
church accommodation'.[19] Three years later in his charge of
1835 Sumner returned to the same theme. 'One area', he said,
where the church has 'manifestly failed is in expanding provision for the needs of the rapidly growing population'.[20] As
Sumner concluded his address he urged as a means of improving the spiritual condition of the people that 'every effort must
be directed to an addition of Church buildings'.[21] He calculated
that a minimum of fifty new churches would be needed each
ten years and fifty clergy to keep pace with the population.[22]

In an effort to achieve this target Sumner became the sponsor and patron of several church building societies within the diocese. In 1834 he organised and founded the *Chester Diocesan Church Building Society*. It had 'the express purpose of encouraging the erection of churches in the more populous parts of the diocese'. Sumner devoted a good deal of energy to preaching on behalf of this society and to organising public meetings and fund-raising events. In June 1838 for example, Sumner preached for the society and noted that since its inception it had erected twenty churches in places where there had been no building previously. In this way 'they had extended the means of salvation to 17,000 souls'.[23] In his address Sumner also bemoaned the fact that 'the society has to depend upon the voluntary offerings of a Christian public'.[24] The bishop's chaplain, Henry Raikes, reported that the society's balance at the end of 1837 was £6,089. 9*s*. 8*d*. The *Chester Diocesan Church Building Society* was supported in all parts of the diocese except in Manchester which had established its own *Manchester and Ecclesiastical Church Building Society*. Early on this society was largely dominated by the 'chapter' of the ancient Manchester parish church.[25]

Alongside these societies, the *Cheshire Building Society* was also formed with the specific object of building chapels in rural districts away from the major areas of industry and commerce. Sumner was also active in promoting the interests and work of this society. He outlined the objective of the society as being 'the urgent provision of small chapels with resident curates, wherever there were townships which were separated from the mother church by a distance of several miles.[26]

Both societies flourished and in his charge of 1838 Sumner reported that during the last three years more than 50 churches had been erected 'in that important district which lies between the Ribble and the Mersey'.[27] Some 32 of them had received their ministries and were offering regular worship and pastoral care. In the following year Sumner gave details of the churches he had consecrated since becoming bishop of the diocese. In 1840 this amounted to 161 new churches which provided 24,047 sittings in Cheshire, 99,037 sittings in Lancashire and

5,670 sittings in Cumberland, and Westmorland. Not only did Sumner promote the building of new churches, he also appointed rural deans under a new patent by which they were to visit churches and to see that they were in a good state of repair.[28]

In the matter of church building Sumner's achievements were remarkable by any standards. A total of 244 new churches were built during his time as bishop. Tribute was paid to his work in this area by Sir Robert Peel in a speech in the House of Commons in May 1843.[29] Among other things he said: '... it would not be just, were I not to express in strong terms, my admiration for the Bishop of Chester who has effected so much improvement in that diocese....'[30] Geoffrey Best described Sumner as 'one of the greatest promoters of new churches and schools'.[31] It is undoubtedly true that Sumner's policy of church building gave a major boost to Christian mission in the diocese. However, it would be idle to deny that criticisms can be made regarding the way in which his policy was implemented. Some of the churches were very large and costly and proved difficult to fill and maintain. For example, St Thomas' Church, Preston was calculated to seat 1,050 people and the new church at Broughton near Manchester had sittings for 1,150 people at a cost of £5,500. Similar criticisms were also made regarding some of the churches which Sumner consecrated in rural areas.

Encouragement of the Clergy

Unlike many earlier nineteenth-century prelates Sumner saw one of his major roles as that of *pastor pastorum*. This was not something which he had to do with conscious deliberation; he had a pastor's heart and took naturally to the task. After being in his diocese for only a year his wife, Marianne, died at Wandsworth[32] in March 1829. Although her loss caused him great sadness, he resolved, as put in a letter to William Wilberforce, 'to forget my own loss and the destitution of my family'.[33] It soon became clear that his diocese and particularly his clergy, had become his family. For almost twenty years Sumner gave himself unstintingly to the task of encouraging and supporting them. He travelled great distances to preach to their congregations, he entertained many of them with gracious simplicity in his home and he arranged meetings[34] where he could hear and learn about their needs and concerns.

Something of John Bird Sumner's meticulous devotion to his clergy can be seen by glancing at his detailed notes on the many parishes of his diocese. They are written in Sumner's own hand and give full details of the number of communicants, Sunday schools, mid-week meetings and relationships with dissenters. Each incumbent's name is written in full and Sumner adds details about their stipends and small pieces of information such as 'his wife is ill'.[35]

Sumner took great care in the preparation and presentation of his diocesan charges. Although he did address himself to national issues such as the Oxford movement and education, he invariably made the task of the clergyman one of his central concerns. In his charge of 1829, Sumner urged on his clergy the need to teach the seriousness of sin and the cross as its only remedy. Men and women, he said, 'need to be convinced... of the sinfulness of sin: to be taught that "the wages of sin is death", eternal death. And the atonement made by the Son of God, the sacrifice of the cross, is the great instrument of working this conviction.'[36] Later in the same charge Sumner asserted: 'A clergyman who has his heart in his profession, is the happiest of men: in the business of his life at least, if not in actual temperament.'[37] As has been stated above, Sumner's episcopate coincided with a period of very rapid population growth in the north-west of the country. He was not only concerned with the difficulties caused by lack of church accommodation, but was equally taxed by the difficulty of attracting sufficient clergy to the diocese. In his charge of 1835 he said: 'We have not multiplied the shepherds, as the flocks became more numerous: we have not added fresh folds, when our enclosures had become too full and overcrowded.'[38]

There were of course a number of difficulties in attracting clergy to the north. The work was demanding, the environment hard and the accommodation frequently inadequate. Equally serious was the fact that many benefices were poorly or inadequately paid.[39] Sumner gave much time to trying to raise the level of endowments and to increasing the salaries of many of the assistant curates. The *Peel Papers* contain a number of letters in Sumner's own hand dealing with these matters. In some he proposed to the *Ecclesiastical Commission for Endowment* the setting up of new district churches.[40] In others, he writes putting forward the names of those he considers to be worthy applicants for the newly created positions. The exchange between Sumner and Sir Robert Peel in December 1845 is fairly typical. Peel wrote from Whitehall on the 10th enclosing a petition he had received from the inhabitants of Ashton-under-Lyme requesting that Thomas Quick be appointed to the newly constituted district of the town to be called the Charleston District. Sumner replied on 14th stating that he believes Mr Quick to be 'a very suitable person for the district'.[41] In his efforts to increase the pay of the assistant curates of his diocese Sumner received much help from *The Church Pastoral Aid Society* of which he was an enthusiastic supporter. In 1838 the Chester diocese was receiving financial grants from the society for more than 30 curates. Another 20 were being funded by *The Additional Curates Society*.[42]

Because of the difficulties of attracting clergy to his diocese Sumner has been accused 'of filling the complement of unbeneficed staff in unpleasant industrial parishes' with 'necessitous ministers of the Irish Church'.[43] In fact in 1837 he was said to have imported no less than 200. There does seem to be some substance to this,[44] but there is no evidence to suggest that the Irish clergy were any less conscientious than their English counterparts or that they proved generally incompetent. Many Irish clergy were extraordinarily eloquent and some worked their way into benefices.

Sumner also devoted himself to the matter of clergy training. He was involved in the establishment of St Aidan's College, Birkenhead in 1846, and gave much support to its first Principal, Joseph Baylee. In addition, Sumner had taken a keen interest in the College at St. Bees which had been founded in 1816. Both institutions had been set up with the specific object of assisting men who could not afford a University education.

In all his work among the clergy of the diocese Sumner was helped and supported by Henry Raikes, whom he had known from his school days at Eton.[45] Raikes, the brother of Robert the Gloucestershire newspaper proprietor and pioneer of Sunday schools, became Chaplain to Sumner in 1828, and in 1830 was made Chancellor of the diocese. Charles Simeon is reputed to have said of this happy partnership: 'The great diocese of Chester enjoys a sort of double episcopacy in the cordial coadjutorship of the Chancellor with the bishop of the see.'[46] Among the senior clerical appointments which were made by Sumner several were convinced Simeonite evangelicals.

Whatever else may be said of Sumner his care and support of his clergy was of a high order. His advice was invariably wise, kindly and gracious. For example, in 1832 he urged clergy not to have Morning Prayer and Evening Prayer so close in time to each other that it was impossible for those who lived at a distance to attend.[47] On another occasion, Sumner, who had a real concern for the poor, urged his clergy not to distribute the alms collected at communion to the poor at the service time. In his view it was leading to the altar some of the most wicked people in the parish.[48] Sumner counselled his clergy to have a vision for the locality in which they exercised their ministry and not to be overly tied to the parish structures which in his view were cumbersome and outdated. 'Our population has outgrown our system', he said, 'our ecclesiastical divisions are imperfect and inconvenient. If we wait till all difficulties are smoothed, we shall wait till the world passes away!'[49] In all of his dealings Sumner stands out as a gracious, dignified yet humble prelate who motivated and inspired his clergy to increasingly dedicated pastoral care and leadership.

Lay Visitors

A third major aspect of Sumner's strategy for his diocese was the training and use of lay visitors to work alongside and assist the clergyman in the care of his parish. In doing this, Sumner was not engaged in a practice which was entirely innovatory, for John Wesley had made good use of both men and women

as lay helpers in the eighteenth century and both the Wesleyan
and the Primitive Methodists were using lay people with considerable effect in Lancashire and Cheshire during the period
of Sumner's episcopate. In Sumner's notes on the parishes of
his diocese there are numerous references to the presence of
nonconformists and the effectiveness of their labours.

In addition to the influence of the Methodists, Sumner would
undoubtedly have witnessed the powerful oratory of many of
the Chartist and Owenite speakers who were active in parts of
his diocese. If laymen could prove so effective in the cause
which some of Sumner's fellow evangelicals regarded as 'the
unclean spirit out of the mouth of the beast',[50] why could they
not be harnessed in the service of Christ's cause? Sumner was
also impressed with Thomas Chalmers' use of lay helpers in the
work of his Glasgow parish. He drew the attention of his clergy
to the 'large and populous town of Brighton'. This, he pointed
out, had for some years been divided into six districts... and has
visitors regularly appointed... some males but chiefly females'.[51]

Sumner first mooted the possibility of lay helpers and visitors in his charge of 1829. Having remarked on the very large
size of the parishes, Sumner declared it was not for the strength
of activity of the clergy alone to provide what was necessary.[52]
He went on to remind them that in the early Church there were
those who were not commissioned to preach as apostles, but
who were nevertheless associated in that task. Paul spoke of
them as 'helpers in Christ Jesus'.[53] Sumner therefore came to
the point by applying this to the situation in the Chester diocese.

> Let the minister of a populous district, using careful discrimi-
> nation of character, select such as 'are worthy' and 'of good
> report', and assign them their several employments under his
> direction: they may lessen his own labour by visiting and
> examining the schools, by reading and praying with the infirm
> and aged, by consoling the fatherless and widows in their
> affliction.[54]

In his next charge of 1832 Sumner referred back to his charge
of 1829 and stated that not only had some of his clergy acted
on his advice, but it had yielded extremely positive results. In
the first year lay helpers had been used in the town of Lancaster,

it had the effect of introducing more than a hundred children to schools that had been short of pupils, and of bringing seventy-nine persons to a regular attendance at public worship, who had been 'living without God in the world'.[55] In the succeeding year 'eighty one more persons were reclaimed by like means, and an hundred and eighteen fresh scholars united to the schools'.[56] In 1832 the Lancashire Visiting Society dealt with the needs of 1,250 families.[57]

A similar visiting Society was established at Chester with equally positive results. At the 1838 Annual General Meeting of the *Chester Visiting Society*, Sumner spoke of 'the excellency of the institution'. He went on to say that 'it armed the poor against sudden overwhelming poverty; and... sent messengers of mercy to visit the abodes of wretchedness, in the hour of affliction.[58] Sumner's plan for visitors was that they should be active in three particular aspects of parish life: visiting, examining schools and care for the needy. A major task of the visiting was to be the reading and explanation of the scriptures. 'Excellent results, far beyond expectation, have been found to proceed from... the simple reading and exposition of Scripture to such a party as can be conveniently assembled in the houses of the poor.' In his charge of 1838 Sumner gave an instance of the remarkable work which could be accomplished by a Scripture visitor. One man had devoted two evenings a week to visiting the Mersey boatmen locally known as 'flatmen' and instructing them in the Scripture.

> Suffice it to say, generally, that our flatmen are as now as remarkable for stability, good order, attention to religious duties, the observance of the Sabbath and... such conduct as eminently adorns the gospel...[59]

In encouraging the work of visiting Sumner was always ready to give practical advice and help. The first thing which the visitor has to do is 'conquer his nose'. Once having established his presence he or she needed to read and expound the Scriptures. Here Sumner provided many plain and useful aids, in particular his *Apostolic Preaching Considered in an Examination of St Paul's Epistles* published in 1815 and later his *A Practical Exposition of the Gospels of St Matthew and St Mark, in the Form of Lectures intended to assist the Practice of Domestic Instruction and Devotion.* Many of Sumner's expositions of the Scriptures proved their popularity by going through several editions.

Inevitably the work of Sumner's visiting Societies has attracted accusations of social control from twentieth-century historians. For example, Geoffrey Best has written that 'they enabled the incumbent to manage a parish as he would in no other way'.[60] The people, he continued, were 'brought under such discipline with more or less success'. It is true that Sumner, in keeping with the majority of his age, believed the hierarchical constitution of Society to be divinely ordered. Nevertheless it is hard to credit that the primary conscious motivation behind his advocacy of visiting Societies was to teach the poor to remain in their appointed stations. In his later social thinking, particularly after the 1834 Poor Law, Sumner increasingly came to the view that the poor should be stirred and encouraged to improve their lot.

In his advocacy of the use of lay assistants and lay visitors Sumner showed himself to be a very forward thinker in what was still essentially a clerical age. He anticipated the work of two great home missionary Societies: *The Church Pastoral Aid Society* and *The London City Mission.* Founded in 1835, both advocated the use of lay assistants in the campaign for Church extension. The only point where Sumner demurred was in the right of such helpers to lead public worship. In his view this ran counter to the teachings of the 23rd Article.[61] The *Church Pastoral Society*, of which Sumner became a Vice-president and an active supporter, kept itself within the Anglican framework, whereas the *London City Mission* was an inter-denominational organisation and later utilised women as helpers.[62]

The Promotion of Education

The fourth significant contribution which Sumner made to the life of his diocese was in the area of education. He was convinced that unless children and young people grew up able to read and write there was little long-term hope of improving their social or spiritual well-being. Sumner was acutely aware of 'the ignorance in which many of our young are brought up'.[63] He attributed this to two major causes. One was 'the low and degraded state of their parents, rendering them totally reckless of their children's welfare'. The other was 'the selfishness of parents, inducing them, or forcing them to increase their means of subsistence by premature employment of their children's labour'.[64] Sumner felt that in the majority of cases the main reason why children were not being educated was not so much the lack of school facilities, but rather that the parents 'do not value it sufficiently'.[65]

In order to make his point more forcibly Sumner published figures for the town of Blackburn which 'shewed that in 1837 the number of children in school was one in five of the whole population'.[66] He also pointed to the situation in the vicinity of Preston which was very much the same.[67]

Sumner's views on education were distinctive. He recognised the weakness of a purely secular education. In a public address of 1838 he stated:

> It is indeed a humiliating fact, though a fact too important to be concealed, that when we have succeeded in obtaining the most cultivated or intellectual man, we have no security that we have obtained the man who is a useful member of the society to which he belongs.[68]

As Sumner saw it, Christianity must be the foundation underpinning all other aspects of education. 'The man who is wise in the things which scripture teaches', he maintained, 'has also that wisdom which is really to be desired for this world'.[69] Sumner felt very strongly that the most crucial time 'for instructing the mind and forming the character' in these principles were the years from ten to fifteen. The problem, however, was that 'we cannot reasonably expect that these years can ever be generally disengaged from labour'.

Sumner did not believe that even if legislation were to be forthcoming it would totally solve the problem. There would still be the problem of profligate parents and idleness on the part of potential scholars. Much also depended on the goodwill of individual employers towards their younger employees.

Where factory owners such as those at Tintwistle Mills on the Cheshire/Derbyshire border were prepared to give their support to educational endeavour, a great deal could be achieved.[70]

After a decade as bishop, Sumner reached the view that schooling and increased educational opportunities were crucial. He made education the central theme of his diocesan charge of 1838. Sumner underlined some of the more positive developments. For example, during the last three years 59 new schools containing 21,960 scholars chiefly in connection with the *National Society* had come into being between Macclesfield and Preston. Nevertheless despite these improvements, the majority of children and young persons enjoyed no such benefit. Sumner therefore urged the clergy to do all in their power to improve the situation. Sumner anticipated the later nineteenth-century Roman Catholics in that he recognised that a school building was often of great value since it could meet the needs of both worship and education. As he wrote:

> It [a schoolroom] is sometimes hardly inferior to a church. The stranger to the church is more likely to enter it than a church. The poor who are unwilling to exhibit their poverty and rags in a church might well enter a schoolroom.[71]

Sumner was a warm supporter of the *National Society*. During his time in Chester he often spoke at services on its behalf and made public appeals for funds. For example, the Revd James Haldane Stewart who ministered in Liverpool from 1831 to 1846, recalled how Sumner came over from Chester to preach in his church in 1835 and 'to assist him in securing funds to establish a National School in the parish'.[72]

In addition to promoting the building of new day schools Sumner's education strategy also developed in other areas. He spent a considerable amount of time encouraging the development of Sunday Schools, and promoting evening classes[73] and he was possibly the major influence behind the founding of the *Chester Training College* in January 1839. In his charge of 1835 Sumner declared that the Sunday School was the only formal education that many people ever had because the early age at which the young resort to daily labour, removes them from the week-day school before they have received much permanent benefit'.[74] Sunday Schools were therefore a vital component in the education of the poor. Sumner was gratified at the progress of the Sunday Schools within his diocese and commended his clergy warmly for their labours.

> The Sunday School is the only resource. And... there is nothing on which the eye can rest with greater satisfaction than on the Sunday-schools, as conducted under our establishment in most of our populous towns; and containing I rejoice to say, in Lancashire and Cheshire, not fewer than 120,000 young persons.[75]

The jewel in the crown of Sumner's educational strategy was to be his major role in the founding of Chester College. The prime mover was Sumner's Chancellor, Henry Raikes,[76] but without his bishop's gracious and good relations with other sections of the wider Church it is doubtful whether the project would have been as successful. Sumner backed the institution because he saw clearly that good teachers would result in larger schools, for 'when parents realised there were good teachers in National schools they would be prepared to pay a little for their children's education'.[77] The decision to found the Chester College was taken at a meeting which Sumner convened at the Adelphi Hotel, Liverpool, on 8 February 1839.[78] The meeting established the membership of the Diocesan Board of Education and appointed a Committee for the Training College 'with power to nominate the Principal to the Bishop and to establish rules and regulations for the College'.[79] The buildings were virtually complete by the close of 1841 at a cost of less than £9,000. It was the first teacher-training College to be built in England. Although there were initial difficulties in raising the necessary capital the College proved to be a highly satisfactory venture. Sumner spoke confidently of it.

> I believe that we have taken the right step in applying ourselves to the education of masters in preparation for the education of our children. And I look to the training College now happily established at Chester and able to send forth its 30 masters annually... as one of the bright stars in the present prospect.[80]

The increase in the numbers being sent out meant that Sumner's hopes of expanding pupil numbers at the schools were able to be realised.[81]

Sumner the Bishop

Sumner's twenty-year tenureship of the episcopate at Chester provides many achievements worthy of comment. He was an astute and clear-thinking strategist. He recognised that no bishop could adequately govern and give pastoral care to so vast an area let alone one in which the population was growing so rapidly. It was during his term of office that the huge and unwieldy diocese was gradually reduced to a more manageable size. Before his translation to the Primacy, Sumner had transferred the archdeaconry of Richmond to the Ripon diocese and assisted in the creation of the new see of Manchester which came into being in 1847.

In an age of rapid social and economic change, Sumner showed himself ready to question, and in some cases challenge, the time-honoured structures of the established church including the parish system. He was ready to experiment with lay workers and with new and simplified forms of worship. He advocated religious gatherings in private houses and the licensing of premises other than church buildings for Sunday services. He was a great promoter of district churches and proprietory Chapels.

Sumner was also immensely hard-working, and travelled about the diocese for months at a time. In his *Memoir of the Rev. Canon James Slade MA Vicar of Bolton* (1892), James Atkinson relates the story of Sumner's arrival in Manchester on St Matthew's Day 1829. The Bishop had apparently been on the move since 4 August on a tour of visitation and confirmation throughout his extensive diocese. Whilst based in Manchester Sumner visited a number of surrounding towns including Bury, Rochdale and Oldham, preaching charity sermons, consecrating new church buildings and confirming many hundreds of candidates. Atkinson gives a detailed account of Sumner's visit to Manchester Collegiate Church where he preached to a crowd estimated 'by some as low as four thousand and by others as exceeding five thousand. Later the same day he went down Deansgate to St Matthew's Church, Campfield, where 1,700 were confirmed.'[82]

During Sumner's period in office 233 new districts and new district churches were formed giving added accommodation for 194,745 persons. The number of clergy increased by 361. Some 671 new day-schools were erected and a great many Sunday schools were improved and strengthened. The result of this growth was seen in a steady increase in those attending church services[83] and rising numbers at Holy Communion Services.[84]

When Sumner's appointment to Canterbury was announced in the Autumn of 1847 there followed many tributes to his immensely valuable work in the Chester Diocese. The Quarterly Meeting of the Mayor, Aldermen and Burgesses and the City Council of Chester presented Sumner with an address in which they expressed 'our deep and unfeigned regret at losing you as a resident in this city'. They went on to single out Sumner's untiring support of all measures 'having for their object the comfort and well being of all classes of our fellow citizens and ameliorating the condition of the unfortunate, the distressed and the destitute. They also expressed their deep appreciation of Sumner's unaffected piety,' his 'humility' and his vigilant defence of 'the principles of the Reformation'.[85] They congratulated his Lordship on 'the attainment of honours which are most worthily accomplished'.[86]

The clergy of the rural deanery of Rochdale expressed their gratitude and respect at Sumner's 'able superintendence of this diocese'.[87] They noted in particular his 'extensive theological attainments', his unwearied zeal' and his promotion of 'sound popular education'.[88] The clergy of the Ashton-under-Lyme rural deanery testified to their deep sense of the energy and faithfulness with which he had discharged the 'various and responsible episcopal duties'.[89] Sumner also received a letter of thanks from the clergy from Liverpool and its neighbourhood,[90] and 'a letter of "affectionate respect" from the Archdeacon, Rural Dean and 275 Clergy from the county of Chester'.[91]

It would be fair to say that in some respects Sumner's episcopate did look back to the eighteenth century. He was a gentleman scholar and the last bishop of Chester to wear the wig. He was a paternalistic figure and believed that the social hierarchy of British Society was divinely appointed. Yet there were many other aspects of Sumner's period of office in Chester which mark him out as an essentially nineteenth-century prelate. He had a deep personal pastoral concern. Like his associate Charles Simeon, he valued preaching and regarded visiting and the education of the poor as of paramount importance. He did not, unlike some of his colleagues on the bench, indulge in an opulent or lavish mode of existence. His time in Chester was marked by a gracious, but modest lifestyle. In short, Sumner emerges as being in some ways a people's prelate. Small wonder therefore that Sir Robert Peel paid him this tribute in the House of Commons:

> It would not be just, were I not to express in strong terms, my admiration of the conduct of the Bishop of Chester who has effected so much improvement in that diocese which has the good fortune to be under his charge, and to witness his example.[92]

Notes

1. Sumner J.B. to the Duke of Wellington. Royal Archives, Windsor, RA 24542. See also Duke of Wellington to Victoria RA 24543.
2. See Congé d'Élire, Letter and Recommendation to the Dean and Chapter (Chester Diocesan Archives) ref. EDD/2574 Box 2.
3. See *Times* (London) 18 September 1828.
4. Morris R.H., *Diocesan Histories: Chester* (London, SPCK, 1895), p. 233.
5. Richardson R.C., *Puritanism in the Diocese of Chester to 1642*, cited by Moore, *op. cit., pp. 40–41*.
6. *Census of Population* 1831.
7. Morris R.H., *op. cit.*, p. 240.
8. Moore E.R., *John Bird Sumner Bishop of Chester 1828–48* (unpublished MA thesis, University of Manchester, 1976), p. 49.
9. *Ibid.*, p. 52.

10. Sumner J.B., *Christian Charity its Obligations and Objects with Reference to the Present State of Society in a Series of Sermons* (London, J. Hatchard & Son, 1841), p. xi.
11. Morris R.H., *op. cit.*, p. 233.
12. See Sumner J.B., *A Charge delivered to the Clergy of the Diocese of Chester at the Triennial Visitation 1832* (London, Hatchard, 1832), p. xliv.
13. *Ibid.*, p. 6.
14. *Ibid.*, p. ii.
15. *Ibid.*, p. vii.
16. Midwinter E.C., *Victorian Social Reform* (London, Longman, 1968), p. 11.
17. See Sumner J.B., *op. cit.*, p. xvii.
18. See Duncombe D., *A List of Churches Consecrated in the Diocese of Chester during the Episcopate of John Bird Sumner 1828–48* (handwritten, 13 November 1872).
19. Sumner J.B., *op. cit.*, appendix 4.
20. Sumner J.B., *A Charge delivered to the Clergy of the Diocese of Chester at the Triennial Visitation 1835* (London, J. Hatchard, 1835), p. 11.
21. *Ibid.*, p. 29.
22. *Ibid.*, p. 32.
23. *Chester Gazette*, 7 June 1838.
24. *Ibid.*
25. See Ward W.R., *Religion and Society in England 1790–1850* (Batsford, 1972), p. 211.
26. *Chester Gazette* 22 December 1836.
27. Sumner J.B., *A Charge Delivered to the Clergy of the Diocese of Chester at the Triennial Visitation in 1838* (London, J. Hatchard and Son, 1838), p. 21.
28. Moore E.R., *op. cit.*, p. 108. See also *The Times* (London) 8 July 1840.
29. *Ibid.*, p. 113.
30. *Hansard* Vol. lxviii 5 May 1843.
31. Best G., *Temporal Pillars* (Cambridge University Press, 1964), p. 163.
32. *Gentleman's Magazine* 1829 (i) 283. See also Davis C.T., *Some Ancient Houses in Wandsworth* (1912), p. 6.

33. Sumner J.B. to William Wilberforce, 16 March 1829 (MS Wilberforce C3, folio 215 Bodleian Library).
34. Sumner J.B., *Handwritten Notes on the Sumner-organised meeting on the Diocese of Chester* (Chester Record Office) MS EDR 5 box 5.
35. *Ibid.*
36. Sumner J.B., *A Charge Delivered to the Clergy of the Diocese of Chester on the Primary Visitation in August and September 1829* (London, Hatchard, 1829), p. 9.
37. *Ibid.*, p. 28.
38. Sumner J.B., *A Charge Delivered to the Clergy of the Diocese of Chester at the Triennial Visitation 1835* (London, J. Hatchard, 1835), p. 14.
39. See Best G.F.A., *The Constitutional Revolution*, cited by Moore E.R., *op. cit.* p. 43.
40. See for example *Peel Papers* (British Museum) Vol. ccclxii MS 40, 54 folios 207; Add MSS 40546 folio 252.
41. *Ibid.*, Vol. ccclxxv folio 356 and 358.
42. Sumner J.B., *A Charge delivered to the Clergy of the Diocese of Chester at the Triennial Visitation in 1838* (London, J. Hatchard, 1838), p. 25.
43. See Ward W.R., *Religion and Society* 1790–1850 (Batsford, 1972), p. 211.
44. Many of the clergy on Sumner's lists appear to have been graduates of Trinity College Dublin.
45. See Raikes, Henry, *Dictionary of National Biography*.
46. *Loc. cit.*
47. Sumner J.B., *Charge 1832*, p. 33.
48. Moore E.R., *op. cit.*, p. 86.
49. Sumner J.B., *Charge 1829*, p. 26.
50. See Lewis D., *Lighten their Darkness* (Greenwood Press, 1986).
51. See Sumner J.B., *Charge 1829*, p. 32.
52. See Sumner J.B., *Charge 1829*, p. 21.
53. *Ibid.*, p. 22.
54. *Ibid.*, p. 23.
55. Sumner J.B., *Charge 1832* p. 9.
56. *Loc. cit.*

57. Ward W.R., *Religion and Society in England 1790–1850* (Batsford, 1972), p. 136.
58. Moore E.R., *op. cit.*, p.146.
59. Sumner J.B., *Charge 1838*, p. 50.
60. Best G.F.A., *Temporal Pillars* (Cambridge University Press, 1964), p. 163.
61. Lewis D., *op. cit.*, p. 245.
62. *Ibid.*, p. 220.
63. Sumner J.B., *Charge 1838*, p. 11.
64. *Loc. cit.*
65. Sumner J.B., *ibid.*, p. 14.
66. Sumner J.B., *Charge 1828*, p. 35.
67. *Ibid.*, p. 36.
68. Sumner J.B., *Charge 1838*, p. 10.
69. *Loc. cit.*
70. *Ibid.*, p. 51.
71. *Ibid.*, p. 62.
72. Stewart D.D., *Memoir of the Life of the Revd J. Haldane Stewart*, (London, J. Hatchard, 1857), p. 249. See also p. 259. For further details of James Haldane Stewart, see Reynolds J.S., *Evangelicals at Oxford* (Marcham Manor Press, 1975), pp. 74, 157.
73. Moore E.R., *op. cit.*, p. 131.
74. Sumner J.B., *Charge 1835*, p. 22.
75. *Ibid.*, p. 22.
76. Bradbury J.L., *Chester College and the Training of Teachers 1839–1875* (Chester College, 1975), p. 25.
77. *Ibid.*, p. 49.
78. *Ibid.*, p. 57.
79. *Loc. cit.*
80. See Sumner J.B., *Charge 1844*.
81. See Bradbury J.L., *op. cit.*, p. 106.
82. Atkinson J.A., *A Memoir of the Revd Canon James Slade MA Vicar of Bolton* (1892), p. 1.
83. Sumner J.B., *Charge 1838*, p. 22.
84. Sumner J.B., *Charge 1832*, p. 33.
85. *Assembly Book* (Chester County Archives), Book 6, p. 728.
86. *Ibid.*
87. *Chester Chronicle* 7 January 1848.

88. *Ibid.*
89. *Ibid.*, 4 February 1848.
90. *Ibid.*, 24 March 1848.
91. *Ibid.*
92. *Hansard*, lxviii, 5 May 1843.

5

Sumner in Parliament

Sumner and Major Social and Political Issues

Sumner took his seat in the Lords making the necessary oaths and declaration on the 9 February 1829.[1] He was thus able to make his maiden speech during the Catholic Emancipation Bill which was introduced into the House in April. On this particular issue Sumner showed himself to be of moderate views. Part of the reason for this moderation may well have been the situation in his own diocese of Chester which had large concentrations of Roman Catholics particularly in Lancashire, together with clusters of Irish immigrants in Liverpool and Manchester. This seems the most plausible explanation for Sumner's taking the opposing view to that of his younger brother Charles and his distinguished University tutor and Cambridge mentor, Charles Simeon.[2] Sumner saw the nub of the issue clearly and wrote as follows to the Duke of Wellington: '... the safety of the whole measure depends very much upon the presumption that the papal cause is a declining cause and will become so more and more.'[3] Had Sumner foreseen the future rapid rise of Roman Catholicism he might not have been so ready to support the measure. However, like others, he clearly saw that the situation in Ireland where roughly eighty per cent of the population were Roman Catholics necessitated the right to elect Roman Catholic members to Parliament. Sumner did not feel that a Roman Catholic Prime Minister would be an insurmountable problem and recommended that in such an eventuality the ecclesiastical functions of the office be put into a commission.[4]

1832 saw the introduction of the Great Reform Bill. Although present for the debates Sumner did not choose to speak. When Lord Grey's Bill was first brought to the House most of the Bishops, including Sumner, voted against it. However, public opinion fuelled by the radical press turned strongly against the bench with the result that some of the more sensitive prelates changed sides. Sumner was amongst their number and voted for the bill on second reading which was carried in the House of Lords on 13 April 1832.[5]

Two years later a significant piece of social legislation came before the house in the shape of the New Poor Law Bill. Until 1834 it had been the practice for individuals who were unemployed to receive money or supplementary payments from the local magistrates. As has been mentioned before, this procedure could lead to unsatisfactory side-effects, and meant that in some cases employers would keep wages at low levels knowing that the parish would supplement them. It also encouraged laziness on the part of some labourers who made little effort to find work, knowing that the parish would provide for them.

Sumner had been a member of the Poor Law Commission which had been sitting since 1832. He accepted the conclusion of the Scottish economist, Adam Smith, who asserted that a man would labour if the individual satisfaction was adequate. For Sumner such satisfaction for the majority of labourers came in the form of a crude materialistic 'love of gain'.

Earlier Sumner had been optimistic that the expanding economy of the post-war years would provide the necessary motivation for the labouring classes. As things turned out, depression set in, bread prices were high and many farm workers resorted to rickburning and rioting under the guise of 'Captain Swing'.[6] By 1826 when he produced his *Evidence of Christianity*, Sumner was beginning to take a very different view stating that 'only the gentle beauties of faith' could provide relief and dignity to 'the lowest stations'. He was particularly dismayed by the rioting and machine smashing by unemployed handloom weavers in several parts of his own diocese. All this caused him to support a bill which led to the establishment of the Workhouse, a much decried aspect of

Victorian England.[7] The New Poor Law required that no able-bodied person was to receive relief except in a workhouse. The country was divided into 600 new Poor Law Unions which ignored the familiar parish basis altogether. Thus many unemployed found themselves not only prisoners in strange new environs but also cut off from the familiar local community.

Although Sumner did not speak during the debate in the House it is clear that his stature as a member of the Poor Law Commission made his informal expressions of support for the Bill an influential factor. The economist Nassau Senior later wrote of Bishop Sumner's role as follows: 'I do not believe that we could have... carried the bill, as it was carried, through the House of Lords, if... the late Bishop Sumner had not supported us.'[8]

The next major piece of social legislation followed a decade later with the repeal of the Corn Laws in 1846. Soloway commented of it: 'Not since the Reform Bill of 1832 had nearly the entire bench been so involved in a non-ecclesiastical piece of legislation.'[9] Sumner and seven Tory Bishops joined with all the Whig prelates in supporting the motion. A number of reasons persuaded Sumner in favour of the bill. As a political economist he was still convinced of the benefits of *laissez-faire* economics and believed that the market should be allowed to find its own level. Like many of the clergy of his industrial diocese, Sumner was sure that the bill was in the best interests of the poor. He also saw the importance of the church siding with a popular opinion which was so obviously rooted in social justice. E. Roy Moore comments on Sumner's position that 'he had fully come to the conclusion that if the Church was to become credible in the eyes of the working classes, the physical and social conditions of the poor must be improved, and the Church not only be seen to be sympathetic, but also active in their welfare'.[10]

One other important area of social concern with which Sumner interested himself was the question of divorce reform. Until the 1850s the dissolution of marriage was only possible by private act of Parliament. In 1850 a Royal Commission on the marriage law was set up and recommended changes which were embodied in Lord Cranworth's Divorce Bill of 1857. The Bill aimed to make divorce more easily attainable and contained a clause to allow the injured wife or husband the right to a divorce. Some bishops held to the sacramental view that marriage was absolutely indissoluble. Others argued that divorce was permissible on the ground of adultery, the so-called Matthean exception clause (Matt. 19:9). Sumner was among their number. In his speech Sumner began by speaking of the danger of increased facilities ending in 'gross laxity of morals'.[11] Sumner appealed to the 'Divine Law' and saying: 'No-one could deny that, according to the general tenor of that law, marriage once contracted, was designed to be indissoluble, saving for one cause—a cause which destroyed the purpose and intent of marriage, the cause of unfaithfulness.'[12] Sumner 'did not see how they could refuse this liberty to an injured wife or husband'. He regretted however that 'the bill did not stop there'. He was deeply unhappy that the guilty parties who had broken an existing marriage could form a new legal union. He roundly declared that:

> ... they would best consult the interests of morality and the comfort of social life if in legislating on this delicate subject they adhered closely to the principle which scripture had laid down. On these grounds while he voted for the second reading of the Bill, he must oppose in committee the clause which permitted the guilty parties to be united in legal marriage.[13]

In the Committee stage a week later Sumner was forthright against allowing the guilty parties to remarry:

> I can neither reconcile it to reason nor to the Divine Command, which is the only safe and proper guide. My Lords, I think that we could hardly furnish a man who desired to possess his neighbour's wife with a more persuasive argument than this clause supplies. I think we could scarcely place a woman dissatisfied with her present lot, in a state of greater temptation, than by consenting to this clause.[14]

Sumner proposed instead an amendment to the effect that only the not-guilty party (the 'party on whose petition the marriage shall have been dissolved') should be legally entitled to remarry. His amendment was carried by a slim majority but subsequently reversed by a further amendment put by the Lord Chancellor. Later in July of the same year when the *Adulterers Second Marriage Bill* was before the house, the proposal was made that such couples who had had a civil ceremony should have 'some sort of religious service afterwards provided a clergyman could be found whose conscience would not be offended by the ceremony'.[15] Sumner's evangelical commitment to scriptural authority made him unequivocal in his opposition. 'Such persons', he declared 'should be satisfied with a civil contract'. He continued, 'It was true charity hopeth all things; but it passed the bounds of charity to pronounce *ex Cathedra*, the Divine approval of a marriage which had its origin in guilty passion, and was brought about by a heinous crime.'[16]

Sumner and Ecclesiastical Issues

Despite taking a prominent part in a number of key social debates, Sumner devoted most of his Parliamentary speeches to Church and Church-related issues. Indeed he spoke on more than thirty such separate bills. His Church-related speeches fall into three main categories: temporalities, doctrine and worship and relationships with other faiths.

Being the bishop of a large diocese with an obvious gift for administration Sumner was always ready to exercise concern for the Church's material assets. During the course of the Pluralities Bill in March 1832 he challenged Lord King to be specific as to those bishops he claimed were pluralists.[17] In the following year the same peer introduced a *Bill for Correcting the Misappropriation of Queen Anne's Bounty*. In his remarks he contended that Church dignitaries were using the money from the Bounty for purposes other than were intended, namely augmenting poor livings. Sumner rose to his feet because he understood a petition complaining about abuses in Chester diocese was being prepared. He stated 'that if ever that petition was presented to their Lordships, he would be perfectly ready to show that it was full of the grossest mis-statements and the greatest ignorance of the subject to which it related.'[18]

These two issues came before the Upper House eighteen years later in the form of the *Ecclesiastical Commission Bill* and the *Benefices in Plurality Bill*. Sumner, who had now been elevated to the primacy, spoke at some length on both matters.

By 1850 the Church Commissioners were dealing with very large sums of money, far in excess of those they had been wont to handle in 1832. It was therefore proposed to appoint three permanent full-time commissioners to manage the church's estates and monies. Sumner spoke strongly in favour of this proposal which was incorporated in the Ecclesiastical Commission Bill. He is reported in *Hansard* as saying:

> It is essential that there should be some responsible officers directly and distinctly charged with the administration of such important affairs, and of such large funds, so that the country might have some large guarantee for the due execution of the one and the due application of the other.[19]

Sumner also took the occasion to defend himself and his fellow bishops against accusations that commissioners' money had gone towards building bishops' palaces: 'episcopal members of the Commission have not been as was supposed, selfish administrators of the means which a great sacrifice on the part of the church has placed in their hands'.[20]

Later in the summer of the same year the *Pluralities Bill* came before the house. This bill proposed to abolish pluralities altogether. Sumner, however, proposed an amendment which provided that an incumbent could hold two benefices in plurality provided that they were 'within three miles of one another by the nearest road, and the annual value of one of which does not exceed £100'. Sumner's thinking was manifestly motivated by his pastoral concerns for the poorest paid clergy. As far as he was concerned it was a basic principle that 'whenever the income of a living was sufficient to support the incumbent, that living was entitled to his services'. Having said that 'their Lordships must regret that the large majority of clergymen were so inadequately remunerated.'[21] Sumner was saddened by the fact that they were now debating 'about a trifling pittance of £100 a year.'[22]

In 1851 Sumner made speeches in two further bills both of which concerned Church temporalities. On both occasions he demonstrated the same concern for the well-being of the Clergy. During the second reading of the *Tithes Assessment and Rent Charges Bill* he expressed his feelings against 'the very marked injustices in the rent assessments of the clergy'. He pointed out that some clergy who lived in large rectories had much lower incomes than some who lived in more modest accommodation. In his view the clergy had good reason for their complaint that no exception was allowed them on account of the personal services which they performed in the local community.

Sumner was very critical of the *Episcopal and Capitular Estates Management Bill* which sought to give the lessees of Church property the right of perpetual renewal. In his view this amounted to possession and might well work to deprive the Church of income which it sorely needed. Sumner had 'great reservations' about the bill but felt strongly that 'the management of Church property might be improved'. He later withdrew his opposition to the second reading of the Bill after receiving assurances that every aspect of the Bill would be scrutinised in the committee stage.

Sumner was not to contribute to any further parliamentary discussions on Church temporalities until February 1860 when Viscount Dungannon inquired whether any Bill was to be proposed in the present session under the sanction of the episcopal bench to amend the laws on glebe and glebe houses.[23] Sumner replied that he had been discussing the matter with his brethren and hoped to be able to introduce a bill shortly. Nothing appears to have been done and Viscount Dungannon again raised the matter in February 1861 inquiring what proposals were in hand regarding the dilapidation of glebe houses. Sumner replied that there was a general wish among the clergy to see this matter settled but there were strongly held differences of opinion, and he could not foresee the possibility of introducing legislation in the immediate future.[24]

By the middle of the nineteenth century there was a strong feeling in some quarters that the Church of England should create an open public forum for debate such as was provided by the Annual Assembly of the Baptist Union. Many churchmen had been deeply troubled by George Gorham's successful appeal on a doctrinal matter to the Judicial Committee of the Privy Council which was a secular court. To the Tractarians in particular this was subjecting the 'divine society' to the judgement of unholy men. As they and their sympathisers saw it, the Church should be free to govern itself.

Promoted by Bishop Samuel Wilberforce and others[25] on the episcopal bench an attempt was made in the Spring of 1851 to revive the custom of allowing the Convocations of York and Canterbury formally to discuss matters of business. Until this time the two Convocations met at the same time as Parliament, but purely as a matter of form. No business could be conducted without the Crown's consent and this had not been given at any time in the previous 135 years.[26]

When Convocation met on 4 February 1851 Bishop Samuel Wilberforce supported by the Bishops of London and Exeter presented a petition urging that some business might be discussed. At this point the Queen's Advocate declared his motion to be illegal and cited the statute of Henry VIII which prohibited Convocation doing business without the express command of the Crown.

However in July of the same year Lord Redesdale introduced a Bill for the Revival of Convocations urging that 'the present state of affairs demanded that the Church provide an open public forum for debate.'[27] He maintained that the Church of England was the only religious community in the Empire to be denied this advantage of public debate and discussion. Sumner was moved to speak out strongly against the bill. He felt that 'the assembling of Convocation with active powers would tend to increase discord in the Church'. He also felt that the nature of the business to be discussed would be 'controversial' and that there would be pleas of 'the liturgy requires revision' or the 'rubrics are inconsistent'. He continued: 'If more were attempted, the doctrine of the Prayer Book were touched, even with the slightest hand, a flame would be lighted up from one end of the country to the other.'

Sumner admitted that Convocation was a very influential body for a hundred years after the Reformation. Nevertheless he asserted that 'it is a mistake to suppose that we owe to that assembly the constitution and fabric of our Church.[28] He pointed out that since 1717 no government had seen fit to advise the sovereign to recall Convocation. Regarding the Free Churches, Sumner argued that they could meet, deliberate and resolve in conference, without causing a national discussion because 'they are not involved in the constitution of the country'.

In all this it could be argued that Sumner showed himself to be a mild and statesman-like primate, albeit not one whose views would find full accord with the democratic leanings of the late twentieth century. With hindsight the bitter wranglings which were later to follow over ritualism and Prayer Book revision could be said to prove him right. However, despite his personal convictions Sumner showed himself to be magnanimous and when in 1852 Lord Derby felt obliged to advise the Queen to allow Convocation both to meet and to discuss business he made no attempt to hinder the proceedings. The necessary arrangements were therefore made enabling the Southern Province to meet in Convocation in 1854 and the Northern in 1861.

Sumner also concerned himself with the Church overseas. He made brief speeches on several issues relating to Anglican developments in the Empire. In May 1852 he moved the second reading of the *Colonial Bishops Bill* which allowed Colonial bishops to officiate outside their diocese when invited to do so.[29] In July 1853 Sumner introduced the *Colonial Church Regulation Bill* which was intended to give the overseas provinces of the Church of England a measure of self-government. The bill provided for the Colonial dioceses to set up assemblies of clergy and laity to frame regulations and exercise discipline, with the proviso that 'no alteration be made in the formularies and articles of our Church'. Sumner spoke of the importance of the Church overseas being able to determine its own conduct and of laymen in particular having 'a considerable share in the

administration of its affairs.'[30] Sumner also took an interest in
a number of bills which were concerned with the Church of
England's relationship with the Free Churches. He spoke in two
debates on the *Burial Bills* which proposed to allow dissenters
the right to have their own pastor to officiate at a funeral service
in the parish churchyard and also addressed the House on the
Church rates question. In both debates Sumner showed himself
to be cautiously in favour of maintaining the *status quo*. He
voted against the *Church Rates Abolition Bill* but earlier he had
stated:

> I am by no means of the opinion that church rates should remain
> as they are, I believe I speak the opinion of those around me
> when I say we should gladly welcome any proposal which
> would be likely to settle this difficult question.[31]

Sumner also spoke during the debate on the *Endowed Schools
Bill* which sought to allow children of dissenters to enjoy the
benefit of endowed schools commonly known as King Edward's Schools. He urged that dissenters' children should be
allowed the opportunities afforded by such schools, but with
the safeguard that no change should be made in their doctrine,
teaching, religious instruction and government.[32]

On other wider social matters Sumner was more forthright.
In April 1852 following various outbreaks of cholera Lord
Shaftesbury moved a resolution 'that the Sanitary State of the
Metropolis required the immediate interposition of Her Majesty's Government'.[33] Sumner rose to his feet in support. 'It
would be impossible', he said, 'not to admire the philanthropy
of the noble earl'.[34] The Archbishop also confirmed the accu-
racy of the Earl of Shaftesbury's assertions in regard to the
conditions in the area of Lambeth which immediately surrounded his palace. In July 1857 Sumner spoke in support of
the *Bill to Prevent the Sale of Obscene Books*. In the course of
the debate it was stated that the *Society for the Suppression of
Vice* under whose prompting Lord Campbell had proposed the
Bill, had successfully prosecuted 154 persons for the publication of indecent literature. Sumner tendered his thanks to Lord
Campbell and those who had made exertions in this cause.

Like all Victorian evangelicals, Sumner also emerges as a keen defender of the Sabbath day as a time for rest and worship. In May 1860 he spoke forcibly against widening the scope of Sunday trading in the debate on the *Selling and Hawking Goods on Sunday Bill.*

In the summer of 1858 Sumner addressed the House in the third reading of the *Government of India Bill.* His speech shows him to be remarkably in advance of the general opinions of his age. He put forward the principle that 'India must be governed in India and not from England', and expressed the view that the Government must not use force to 'overthrow the false religion with which unhappily, we have to deal, or to establish that which we know to be true'.[35] He also insisted that 'no distinction of caste be any longer recognised by the Government' and that 'the British administration should have no part with the rites and customs of an idolatrous religion'.[36]

Throughout his Parliamentary career Sumner's views continued to bear the stamp of his evangelical churchmanship and his adherence to liberal social and economic theories. On matters of religious principle and doctrine he was generally conservative and had a tendency to argue for the maintenance of the *status quo.* This is well illustrated by his cautious attitude to divorce and remarriage, church rates and the burials controversy which we have touched on previously. On the other hand in matters of social or economic concern, or in relation to political issues Sumner was often liberal and on occasions in advance of the received opinion of his peers. Another example of this tendency came in the position he took in regard to the *Catholic Emancipation Bill* which came right at the beginning of his time in the House, and as we have seen above the same tendency can be seen in the views which he expressed at the end of his career towards the *Government of India Bill.* As a member of the Upper House Sumner clearly took his Parliamentary duties seriously. From Parliamentary records he would appear to have been present at most major votes whenever his other commitments allowed and whenever he judged the issue involved to touch upon his responsibilities. For example in 1847, his penultimate year as Bishop of a very large industrial diocese, Sumner still found time to be present in the House on fifteen out of a total of 93 days of Parliamentary debate. His speeches betray the marks of considerable reflection based upon careful preparation. He was motivated always by his strong evangelical convictions, and these working in conjunction with his firmly held belief in *laissez faire* economics shaped his attitudes to most questions. Sumner was present in the House for all the major religious and social debates which took place during his episcopate. He addressed the House on 52 separate occasions. Some of his speeches, particularly those which related to issues with political and religious implications, were lengthy and forcefully argued. With two or three possible exceptions, all of his speeches were on issues which were overtly related to the Church or the Christian faith. When Sumner died the *Record* spoke of 'the high consideration in which he was held in the House of Lords' where he always spoke with dignified simplicity, always to the purpose, and always with effect.'[37]

Notes

1. *Hansard*, 9 February 1829.
2. See Sumner G.H., *Life of R.C. Sumner* (John Murray, 1872), p. 158: also Carus W., *Memoirs of the Life of Rev. Charles Simeon MA* (Hatchard, 1848), p. 443. Simeon expressed grave misgivings about the bill.
3. Chadwick O., *The Victorian Church* (A. & C. Black, 1966), Part 1, p. 10.
4. *Ibid.*, Part II p. 18.
5. J.B. Sumner to Edward Locker 29 December 1832. His change of opinion was clearly influenced by the radical and decidedly whiggish' atmosphere of his new diocese. He wrote in December to a friend: 'For my part, I saw so much of the true Tory breed in the last session that I think but ill of them and believe that mankind would never improve under their influence'.
6. See Gash N., *The Rural Unrest in England in 1830 with Special Reference to Berkshire* (unpublished BLitt thesis, University of Oxford, 1934).

7. Recent research (in particular the work of A. Digby) has led to a reappraisal of the traditional horrific picture of the workhouse.

8. Blomfield A.R. *A Memoir of Bishop Blomfield* (John Murray, 1863), Vol. I, p. 204.

9. Solway R., *Prelates and People 1783–1852* (Routledge and Kegan Paul, London, 1969), p. 222.

10. Moore E.R., *John Bird Sumner, Bishop of Chester 1828–48* (unpublished MA thesis, University of Manchester, 1976), p. 203.

11. *Hansard* Vol. CXLV, 19 May 1857.

12. *Ibid.*

13. *Ibid.*

14. *Ibid.*

15. *Hansard* Vol. CXLVI, 2 July 1857.

16. *Ibid.*

17. *Hansard* Vol. XI, 23 March 1832.

18. *Hansard* Vol. XI, 12 March 1833.

19. *Ibid.*

20. *Ibid.*

21. *Ibid.*

22. *Ibid.*

23. *Hansard* Vol. CLVI, 10 February 1860.

24. *Ibid.*, Vol. CVXI, 5 February 1861.

25. Wilberforce R.G., *Life of the Right Reverend Samuel Wilberforce* (John Murray, 1880–82), Vol. 2, p. 136.

26. *Ibid.*

27. *Hansard* Vol. CXVIII, July 1851.

28. *Ibid.*, Vol. CXVIII.

29. *Ibid.*, Vol. CXXII, 4 May 1852.

30. *Ibid.*, Vol. CXXIX, July 1853.

31. *Ibid.*, Vol. CLI, 2 July 1858.

32. *Ibid.*, Vol. CLVI, January 1860.

33. *Ibid.*, Vol. CXX, 29 April 1852.

34. *Ibid.*

35. *Ibid.*, Vol. CLI, July 1858.

36. *Ibid.*

37. *The Record*, 8 September 1862.

6

Opponent of
the Oxford Movement

On 14 July 1833 John Keble preached his celebrated 'Assize Sermon' in the University Church at Oxford.[1] Although it was intended that the sermon be addressed to judges of the King's bench, Keble's celebrated address was entitled 'National Apostasy'. To Keble and his friends it seemed as if the English nation was falling away from its Christian foundation. Their claim was based upon their view that the English nation and in particular the English Government, no longer appeared to have full regard for its national Church. The sermon was preached against the immediate background of the Whig government's *Church Temporalities Act*[2] which suppressed ten out of 22 Irish bishoprics. There were however other factors which were causing high churchmen considerable alarm. In 1828 the government had removed the formal prohibition on nonconformists taking office on town councils and had allowed Roman Catholics to become MPs by the *Emancipation Act of 1829*. Whilst it had been the case for some time that nonconformists could become MPs, the new act could be seen as leading to the point where more and more non-members of the Church of England were effecting the Church's affairs. Added to this was the rising tide of the liberal spirit which helped to prompt the *Reform Act of 1832*.

The men of the Oxford Movement set themselves the task of rescuing the established Church from the floodtides of liberalisation and secularism. A major part of their solution was

theological. They sought by means of the doctrine of Apostolic
Succession to demonstrate that the Church of England was part
of the one 'true' Holy Catholic and Apostolic Church. This
doctrine maintained that through an unbroken line of bishops
beginning from the apostles, the divine grace of apostolic order
was passed down to succeeding generations through the laying
on of hands. The episcopate of the Church of England, it was
claimed, was a branch of this direct line because at the Reformation her bishops were within the Catholic Church. John
Henry Newman articulated this doctrine in Tract I. As he wrote:
'The Lord Jesus Christ gave his Spirit to His Apostles, they in
turn laid their hands on those who should succeed them; and
then again on others; and so the sacred gift has been handed
down to our present bishops.'[3]

In order to establish the Catholic nature of the Church of
England more firmly in the minds of the British public, the
Tractarians began to study the first centuries of the undivided
Catholic Church. Here they re-discovered the roots of many
medieval practices and beliefs such as elemental change in the
substance of the bread and wine at Communion, the practice of
fasting and daily prayer, special respect for the Virgin Mary,
prayers for the departed, an emphasis on the mystical understanding of God and the suggestion that justification included
actions as well as faith in Jesus Christ.[4]

Keble, Newman, Pusey and their associates began gradually
to introduce these practices and beliefs into the life of the
Church of England. Inevitably, evangelical churchmen of the
Claphamite and Recordite groups took offence. As they saw it
the Tractarians were attempting to unravel the Reformation
settlement on which the Church of England rested. John Bird
Sumner rapidly emerged as one of the most outspoken critics
of the Oxford Movement, and he was the first bishop to con-
demn the 'Tracts' explicitly.[5] In his Charge of 1838 Sumner
denounced those who were bringing about 'a revival of the
worst evils of the 'Romish System'.[6] He continued:

> Under the specious pretence of deference to antiquity, and
> respect for primitive models, the foundations of our Protestant
> Church are undermined by men who dwell within her walls,

and those who sit in the Reformers' seat are traducing the Reformation. It is again becoming a matter of question whether the Bible is sufficient to make a man wise unto Salvation.[7]

In 1841 Newman published his celebrated *Tract Ninety* in which he attempted to show that the *Thirty-Nine Articles* were not hostile to the Church of Rome. This provoked widespread antagonism among the bishops against the Tractarians. John Bird spoke of the writers as 'instruments of Satan to hinder the true principles of the Gospel'.[8] He made the 'erroneous' teaching of the Tractarians the central theme of his charge of 1841. He summed up his feelings on the matter in the following lines.

> We could not, in this land of light, maintain the fatal claims which the Romish priests assume, and which nothing except the darkness in which they shroud their people could enable them to preserve. We pity them, whether deceivers or deceived: God forbid that we should either imitate or envy them.[9]

Following his attack on the teachings of the Tractarians, Sumner received an address signed 'by a large number of lay members of the Church of England in the town and neighbourhood of Blackburn'.[10] It was printed in the *Times* of 22 September 1843. Not only did these inhabitants express 'their highest satisfaction and admiration' of Sumner's indefatigable and truly apostolic devotion to the arduous duties of your sacred office' but they continued:

> ... to acknowledge our lasting obligations to your Lordship for your firm, consistent, and uncompromising resistance to the system of those tractarian divines who—true to their self-assumed title of 'ecclesiastical agitators'... left the Church... with the avowed object of 'unprotestantising the national Church' by receding 'more and more from the principles of the English Reformation'.[11]

Sumner replied from Durham in a letter dated 12 September 1843 which he sent to James Neville, the chief signatory. He thanked the group for their support and 'rejoiced' in 'the proof it affords that the principles established by our reformers are dear to so many hearts'.

Justification

For all Protestant-minded evangelicals the central Christian doctrine was 'Justification by faith alone', as clearly expressed in Article 6 of the *Thirty-Nine Articles*. As Sumner put it: 'This is the fundamental and characteristic article of all the Reformed Churches: laid as it were as their corner-stone: that we are accounted righteous before God through the merit of Christ alone, and not "or our own works or deservings".'[12]

In his diocesan charge of 1841 Sumner identified as one of the major dangers confronting the National Church the obscuring of this crucial doctrine.[13] Such, he said, had been 'in all ages and countries'. Even Paul had to grieve over the disciples in Galatia that they were 'removed from the grace of Christ into another gospel.'[14] Referring to the present crisis provoked by the Oxford Movement Sumner declared:

> Those have now risen up who affirm that the doctrine of the Gospel, the propitiation made for sin, is a doctrine too dangerous to be disclosed, too mysterious to be generally exhibited; and would thus deprive the sinner at once of his motive to repent and his comfort in repenting.[15]

Sumner expressed the doctrine of justification in the Solifidean terminology of Luther. He is emphatic that there is only one way to possess the Son and that is by 'believing in Him'.[16] Sumner laboured this same point at considerable length in his *The Doctrine of Justification Briefly Stated*[17] which he published in 1843. Having set out what is meant by justification in the first section of the book, Sumner considered how it can be appropriated in the life of the believer.

> The benefit is to be obtained by... Faith within... so the Lord declared: 'He that heareth my word, and believeth on him that sent me, hath everlasting life'.... 'I am the resurrection and the life: he that *believeth* on me... shall never die.'[18]

In a subsequent paragraph Sumner cited the conversion of the Ethiopian official as a paradigm for laying hold of justification.

> He perceived that what he needed was in Christ Jesus; that peace with God was to be procured through his propitiation; he

believed that Jesus was the Son of God, 'the Lamb of God, which taketh away the sins of the world'. And thus he was accounted righteous before God.[19]

Sumner made the same point very succinctly in his charge of 1841. 'By one way alone', he declared, 'can man possess the Son that is by believing in him'.[20] Sumner also underscored Luther's point that this faith is a gift. It must not be understood 'as if faith were a work of obedience'.[21]

One of the fundamental disagreements which evangelicals such as Sumner had with the Tractarians was the place of works in justification. Numbers of the Oxford men were returning to the medieval notion that justification was a lifelong process maintained and nurtured by good works. Sumner followed Luther and the Protestant reformers and asserted that our works can make no contribution whatsoever towards our acceptance by God. Good works do nevertheless flow out from the justified life.

Sumner argued that the Roman Church confused two things, 'what has been done for us', namely Christ's sacrifice for sin, and 'what is being done in us' Christ's working in the believer's life. If a man puts hope in this second aspect he is 'induced to look to himself, and not to his Redeemer, for acceptance with God'.[22] Sumner demonstrated the futility of such reliance by making the point that our own righteousness is an 'imperfect righteousness'.

> There is a righteousness which is inherent, and a righteousness which is not inherent. The righteousness whereby we are sanctified, is inherent, but not perfect. The righteousness whereby we are justified, is perfect, but not inherent. This is the fundamental and characteristic article of all the Reformed Churches: laid as it were their corner-stone; that we are accounted righteous before God through the merits of Christ alone, and not 'for our own deserving'.

Sumner demonstrated the force of his argument by stating that 'if works are to contribute to justification 'then grace is no more grace'. Or again he maintained that if man can assist in his salvation then he is not a corrupt being who needs redemption.[23] He summed up the matter as follows in his *Doctrine of Justification Briefly Stated*: 'to follow what is, in effect, the Romish system, and unite together two things so distinctly separated in the Christian scheme, as man's Justification and his Sanctification, is in effect to devise a scheme of salvation for ourselves'.[24]

Although like the Reformers Sumner was vehement that our works play no part in our justification with God he followed them in maintaining that good works are the fruit of true faith. Put simply, he believed that works will not justify a man in God's sight, but good works are the fruit of faith. Answering the 'erroneous' teaching of the Tractarians in the charge of 1841, Sumner asserted that a man is:

> ... not accepted with God, because he is a new creature, but because Christ has made atonement for the wrath which in his old nature he had incurred. His faith in that atonement which led to his acceptance, leads also to his doing works meet for one who is accepted: but the works which follow his being justified, and are its effect, can never also be the cause of his justification.[25]

These works are a simple token of the believer's 'gratitude to the physician whose remedy has justified him and brought him wholeness'. In his *Doctrine of Justification Briefly Stated* Sumner is emphatic that a man justified by faith is not exempt and or cannot consider himself free from the obligation to obedience. 'Our Lord', he wrote did not set his disciples free from the obligations of duty.... Neither does St Paul exempt the Roman Christian from the obligation of holiness.'[26]

In 1843 Sumner took material from his *Practical Exposition of St Paul's Epistle to the Romans* and moulded it into a Tract for the Times which was subsequently accepted by *SPCK's Tract Committee*. A Tractarian sympathiser who was another member of the Society, the Revd William Dodsworth, objected strongly to the tract on grounds that it was 'ultra-Lutheran and Sectarian and opposed to Holy Scripture, the Creed, the Articles and Ritual of the Church of England, as well as the sentiments of the founders of the *Society for Promoting Christian Knowledge*'.[27] Sumner replied to Dodsworth through the means of his charity sermon preached at the benevolent Institution, the *Female Orphan Asylum*'.[28] Among other things Sumner sought to demonstrate that the doctrine of Justification by Faith is 'not opposed to the fruits of holiness in the heart and life.' On the contrary Sumner emphasised the importance of having faith in Christ because:

> ... if you believe in the heart that Jesus was delivered for your offences, and raised again for your justification: then we have little need to inculcate Charity, for it will be part of your faith that you... glorify your Redeemer with your heart and with your substance, which are his.[29]

Dodsworth regarded Sumner's views as a threat to the Society. In 1844 he published *An Appeal to the Members of the Society for Promoting Christian Knowledge on Doctrinal Changes lately introduced into a series of Tracts circulated under their Authority*.[30] In it he maintained that Sumner's tract would reduce the SPCK 'to the level of the Bible Society and the Religious Tract Society'.[31] The *Christian Observer* responded that 'far from Dr Sumner introducing novelty no group have more specialised in this 'than Mr Dodsworth's good friends the Tractarians'.[32]

Baptism

Another area in which the Tractarians caused controversy was that of baptism. As with other doctrines they began to return to medieval notions. Their sentiments were expressed in hymns such as We love the Sacred font, For there the Holy Dove pours out as He is wont, His 'blessing from above'. In particular they began to see infant baptism as the instrumental cause of regeneration. Pusey who set out the Oxford movement's position at length in Tracts 67–69, which could happily speak of baptism 'washing away sin'. Sumner's earliest views on baptism were not typically evangelical. In his early work entitled *Apostolic Preaching* which he published in 1815 Sumner had noted that the Church of England teaches that baptism 'conveys regeneration'.[33] In later years particularly those after the emergence of the Oxford Movement, Sumner moved away from this position and emphasised faith as the necessary pre-requisite to regeneration. In 1843 in his study of justification Sumner cited Philip as a model of baptism. He 'believed that Jesus was the Son of

God, which taketh away the sin of the world'. Therefore he claimed to himself the benefit in the prescribed way being baptised in the name of the Lord'.[34] In a footnote, Sumner anticipated the question, 'why then are infants baptised when by reason of their tender age they cannot believe?' In his answer to them he declared that there is no suggestion that such infants will automatically have regeneration conveyed to them. On the contrary 'they promise faith by their sureties'.[35] In 1859 Sumner published *Practical Reflections on Select Passages of the New Testament*. In this volume he includes a number of passages on the meaning of baptism. In them he makes it explicitly clear that in his view the mere reception of the Sacrament does not confer grace. 'A man may be', he wrote, 'as it is to be feared multitudes are, baptised, but not regenerate'.[36]

The Church

The first generation of the Oxford Movement had their roots in the High Church Party. It therefore was no surprise that they began to develop a 'high' view of the Church. They saw the Church of England as being in direct descent from the undivided Church of the first four Christian centuries. Newman spoke early on of the Church of England as the 'divine society' and the Oxford leaders tended to identify the local Church and the mystical body of Christ as being one and the same. Later Tractarians claimed that men are joined to 'Christ by being joined to His Church'.[37] The Church as the body is thus the extension of the incarnation. From this it became only a small step to assert that the Church was the instrument or mediator of salvation. The Oxford Movement therefore developed a high view of the visible episcopal Church. As they saw it, it was one and the same as Christ's mystical body.

Sumner, like others of the evangelical party, was not unnaturally concerned about these developments. He warned that such a view of the Church is 'injurious to the Saviour's glory'. He continued:

> Practically he is treated with dishonour, when the Church which he has established is made to usurp his place, to perform his

acts, to receive his homage: is so represented as to be, virtually the author of salvation, instead of the channel through which salvation flows.[38]

By this process, as Sumner perceived it, the church is not only 'invested with divinity', but the ministry 'as her visible representative' has 'assumed the place of God'.[39] Far from allowing the tractarian identification of the local congregation with mystical body of Christ, Sumner was adamant in the words of Article 19 that the visible Church of Christ is a congregation of faithful men in which the pure word of God is preached, and the sacraments be duly administered according to Christ's ordinance'.[40] He underlined the work of the Reformers which divested the Church of the mystery in which the medieval period had shrouded it and presented it to the world as 'the company of the believers'.[41] Sumner's view of the church' was typically an evangelical one. He drew a clear distinction between the mystical body of Christ, 'the one holy Catholic apostolic church', and the visible local church. As he saw it, by no means all members of the local visible episcopal church were members of Christ's true church. This church 'continues in the apostle's fellowship', it maintains 'in purity the doctrines and institutions of the Gospel' and it proclaims that 'Christ alone is "the way the truth and the life"', through which every individual member of the Church must seek access to God".[42]

The Ministry

The Oxford Movement also inherited a high view of the Church's ministry. Newman declared that every bishop of the Church whom we behold is 'a lineal descendant of St Peter and St Paul after the order a spiritual birth'.[43] Tractarians never doubted that the episcopate was of the *esse* of the Church. It was ordination by valid bishops which guaranteed the order of presbyters who were thus capable of rightly ministering sacraments which conveyed God's regenerating grace. Thus even in the first phase of the Oxford movement, the clerical office was seen as primarily a sacramental one. Sumner's view of episcopacy was a relatively high one. He saw his office as being in

direct succession 'from those whom Christ Himself had commissioned'.[44] There is no suggestion in any of his writings
however that he understood his office to make up the fullness
of the church or that without episcopacy the church would cease
to have her being. He saw his role primarily as a spiritual leader
and *pastor pastorum* to the clergy of his diocese. He warned
against those clergy who 'so magnify the ministrations belong-
ing to their office, as virtually to represent that, except through
their instrumentality, there is no salvation?[45] Sumner stressed
to his clergy that the role of the ministry was a teaching one.
'The greatest joy of an apostle is', he declared, 'when his
children walk in the truth.'[46] He exhorted the clergy of his own
Chester diocese to take heed to their doctrine and 'to preach the
word, to be instant in season and out of season, to testify, both
publicly and from house to house, repentance towards God, and
faith towards our Lord Jesus Christ; this is to be the successor
of the apostles'.[48]

It was because John Bird saw his clergy in this light that he
was resistant to any suggestion of their wearing forms of
clerical dress which might either detract from the servant nature
of their office or associate them with 'Romish priests'. In his
first year as Archbishop of Canterbury he received a communication from a group of Plymouth clergy who were unhappy
about the requirement by their diocesan bishop that they wear
a surplice when preaching rather than the traditional black
gown. Although he felt unable to intervene he wrote to them
'rejoicing' to find Reformation principles 'sincerely professed
and manfully upheld'.[48]

Supported for his anti-Tractarian Views

Although John Bird received harsh criticism from those whose
sympathies were with the Oxford Movement he received widespread support from the clergy and laity of his diocese. In the
autumn of 1843 Sumner received an address from 'the members
of St George's, Bolton and its neighbourhood'.[49] They took their
stand against those who 'engender prejudice against the Reformation'.[50] The address went on to praise 'your Lordship' for 'a

noble example of devoted attachment to Scriptural truth, by
writing and exhorting against the pernicious opinions of the
Oxford Tractarians'.[51] To his supporters in Bolton Sumner
wrote that he was gladdened by what he saw as 'a proof of your
earnest interest in the cause of evangelical truth'.[52]

The men with whom Sumner worked most closely and in
whom he placed his confidence during the early phase of the
Oxford Movement were men of Protestant convictions. He
appointed his long-standing friend and fellow evangelical,
Henry Raikes (1782–1854), as his chancellor. His first appointment as Archdeacon of Chester was James Hodson, an intimate
of Charles Simeon.[53] Many of the parochial clergy Sumner
appointed were Irish protestants some of whom appear to have
been the cause of tension with the Irish Roman Catholic com-
munities in Liverpool and Manchester.[54] The appointment in
1845 of the Revd Hugh McNeil and the Revd Hugh Stowell as
honorary canons of Chester was seen by the *Times* as in part
due to their protestant stance.[55] Stowell had in fact published
two volumes of sermons entitled *Tractarianism Tested by Holy
Scripture* and *The Church of England in a Series of Sermons*
both of which earned Sumner's warmest approbation.[56] When
Sumner's elevation to the primacy was announced the Council
of the City of Chester held a special meeting for the purpose of
presenting him with an address. The text spoke of 'our deep
regret at losing you as a resident in this city'.[57] Amongst other
expressions of praise they stated 'our sincere belief that a more
vigilant defender of the principles of the Reformation than your
Lordship is not to be found within the pale of the establishment'.[58] The *Christian Observer* commenting on his appointment to Canterbury voiced a similar sentiment that he would
'firmly uphold the principles and doctrines of the Reformation'.[59]

Notes

1. See for example Newman J.H., *Apologia Pro Vita Sua* (OUP, 1964
   edition), p. 36.
2. See Chadwick O., *Victorian Church* (London, A. & C. Black,
   1970), Part 1, p. 56 f.

3. Newman J.H., Tract 1, *Thoughts on the Ministerial Commission* in Hutchinson W.G. (ed.), *The Oxford Movement Being a Selection from Tracts for The Times* (Walter Scott Publishing Co. Ltd., London, 1906), p. 8.
4. *Ibid.*, Tract 38, *Via Media No. 1*, p. 161.
5. Fowler M., *Some Notable Archbishops of Canterbury* (London, SPCK, 1895), p. 159. See also Church R.W., *The Oxford Movement* (McMillan & Co., 1892), p. 251.
6. Sumner J.B., *A Charge delivered to the Clergy of the Diocese of Chester at the Triennial Visitation in 1838* (London, J. Hatchard & Son, 1838), p.6.
7. *Ibid.*, p. 6.
8. Church R.W., *Op. cit.*, p. 25.
9. Sumner J.B., *A Charge delivered to the Clergy of the Diocese of Chester at the Visitation in 1841* (London, J. Hatchard & Son, 1841), p. 42.
10. *The Times* (London) 22 September 1843.
11. *Ibid.*
12. Sumner J.B., *op. cit.*, p. 25.
13. *Ibid.*, p. 20.
14. *Ibid.*, p. 21.
15. *Ibid.*, p. 22.
16. *Ibid.*, p. 23.
17. Sumner J.B., *The Doctrine of Justification Briefly Stated* (London, J. Hatchard & Son, 1843), pp. 13–15.
18. *Ibid.*, p. 13.
19. *Ibid.*, p. 15.
20. Sumner J.B., *Charge 1841* (London, J. Hatchard & Son, 1841), p. 23.
21. Sumner J.B., *Justification*, p. 18.
22. Sumner J.B., *Charge 1841*, p. 22.
23. *Ibid.*, p. 25.
24. Sumner J.B., *Justification*, p. 23.
25. Sumner J.B., *op. cit.*, p. 24.
26. Sumner J.B., *Justification*, p. 22.
27. Dodsworth W., *An Appeal to the Members of the Society for Promoting Christian Knowledge* (London, 1844), p. 29.
28. *Christian Observer*, January 1844.

29. *Ibid.*, p. 8.
30. See note 27.
31. Dodsworth W., *op. cit.*, p. 57.
32. *Christian Observer*, January 1844.
33. Sumner J.B., *Apostolic Preaching Considered* (8th ed., London, J. Hatchard & Son, 1839), p. 160.
34. Sumner J.B., *Justification*, p. 15.
35. *Ibid.*, pp. 15–16.
36. Sumner J.B., *Practical Reflections on Select Passages of the New Testament* (London, J. Hatchard & Son, 1859).
37. See Toon P., *Evangelical Theology 1833–56* (London, Marshall, Morgan & Scott, 1979), p. 172 ff.
38. Sumner J.B. *Charge 1841*, p. 30.
39. *Ibid.*, p. 31.
40. *Ibid.*, p. 32.
41. *Ibid.*
42. *Ibid.*, pp. 33–4.
43. Newman J.H., *Parochial Sermons*, Vol. III, pp. 268–70.
44. Sumner J.B., *op. cit.*, p. 17.
45. *Ibid.*, p. 36.
46. *Ibid.*, p. 43.
47. *Ibid.*, p. 43.
48. *British Magazine*, February 1849.
49. *The Times* (London), 22 September 1843.
50. *Ibid.*, 22 November 1843.
51. *Ibid.*
52. *Ibid.*
53. See Carus W., *Memoirs of the Life of the Rev. Charles Simeon MA* (London, J. Hatchard & Son, 1848), p. 553.
54. See Ward W.R., *Religion and Society in England 1790–1850* (Batsford, 1972), p. 211.
55. *The Times* (London) 29 July 1845.
56. Marsden J.B., *Memoirs of the Life and Labours of the Revd Hugh Stowell MA*, (Hamilton Adams & Co., 1868), p. 154.
57. Meeting of the Council of the City of Chester 28 February 1848, *Assembly Book* 6 (Chester City Archives), p. 746.
58. *Ibid.*
59. *Christian Observer*, March 1848.

7

Claphamite Pastor and Prelate

From his earliest days Sumner was a convinced member of the evangelical party. The term 'evangelical' seems first to have been used of the followers of Martin Luther during the Reformation.[1] Since that time there had been a number of 'evangelical' movements in Britain, beginning in the Cromwellian period, but then subsequently under the influence of such figures as Baxter, Bunyan and Wesley. Whilst only the last of these men had founded his own movement, all of them were highly influential in the development of an evangelical outlook in Britain. From the middle of the eighteenth century until about 1860 'evangelicalism' seems to have become more clearly defined, and started to exhibited several distinctive characteristics. These characteristics have been variously described by recent commentators including Bebbington, Hilton and Hylson Smith.[2] Bebbington for example, states that there were four essential elements: 'conversionism', 'activism', 'biblicism' and 'crucicentrism'.[3]

Evangelical conversionism during this period had several central aspects. First, it was invariably preceded by acknowledgement of wretchedness, guilt and personal sinfulness. Secondly, this initial stage was shortly followed by a realisation of peace and forgiveness through what Hilton calls 'the all important contractual relationship' with Christ. Thirdly, this relationship with Christ was made a reality by the internal witness of the Holy Spirit. This latter aspect of the evangelical movement derived from the work of the Wesleys. They brought a new dimension of assurance to the doctrine of conversion. For them

conversion was not seen primarily in terms of intellectual assent
to sound doctrine, or in subsequent good works which could be
inspected, it was experienced in the heart. What Wesley termed
'personal religion' came to be at the centre of this conversionism. Such conversion tended to be sudden among the Methodists, but Anglican evangelicals set less store by this aspect of it.
Charles Simeon, their leader, once retorted: 'We require nothing
sudden.'

Crucicentrism denotes the view held by evangelicals that
Christ died as a substitute for sinful mankind. This was the sole
basis of justification or being made right with God. Justification
was God's declaration of acquittal to the sinner on the sole basis
of Christ's actions. As far as Evangelicals were concerned what
Christ had done in the believer, namely sanctification, made no
contribution to justification and came after it. Nor did baptism
or any other sacramental act as some tractarians began to assert
in the 1840s.

'Biblicism' refers to the evangelicals' devotion to the Bible.
They believed it to be unique and divinely inspired. Few held
to dictation theories which bypassed the biblical writers' struc-
turing and expression of the material, however they did consider the Bible to be the sole source of the doctrine of salvation.
This did not mean that they all held eccentric views, or were
extreme literalists in the way in which they interpreted the text.

The 'activism' of evangelicalism sprang from the conviction
of personal accountability. In many evangelical households the
text which hung over the mantelshelf was 'Thou God seest me.'
Evangelicals believed themselves answerable to God for the
way in which they spent every moment of the day. This meant
that they threw themselves wholeheartedly into preaching
and works of philanthropy. There was little time for rest or
relaxation.

These then were the features which marked out Evangelicalism as a distinctive phenomenon during the period from the
middle of the eighteenth to the middle of the nineteenth century.
It was a movement which embraced both protestant noncon-
formity and portions of the established Church.

Within nineteenth-century evangelical anglicanism it is possible to see two distinctive strands. Early Anglican evangelicalism
had its roots in the activities of John Venn, William Wilberforce
and the Clapham Sect. Their stance was broad-based and issued
in generous open-hearted social action. It was reflected in the
Christian Observer journal which the group founded in 1806.

In the 1820s a second and somewhat more introverted form
of evangelicalism began to emerge. It revealed among other
things a predilection for pre-millennial theology, the study of
prophecy and laid emphasis on emotional religious fervour. Ian
Rennie and others date this from the time when Robert Haldane
took up the editorship of the newly formed *Record*. During the
1830s the 'Recordites' moved increasingly towards a narrow,
withdrawn posture in relation to the surrounding culture. In
later years it did battle with Darwin, biblical criticism and
ritualism. Boyd Hilton has distinguished helpfully between
these two groups whom he styles the 'Clapham Moderates' and
the 'extremists'.[4] The moderates preached 'Christ and Him
crucified'. The 'extremists' preached the same but stressed also
'Christ coming very soon'. The Clapham school generally took
a more cheerful view of private and national misfortune,[5]
believing that in many cases it was the result of the natural
consequences of misguided human actions or errors. The 'extremists' on the other hand sometimes appeared to welcome
disaster as a sign of the coming of the last days[6]. The moderates
generally had a more cheerful and affirming attitude to the
pleasures of living than the extremists. They were sometimes
post-millennialists who saw the need to build towards the new
Jerusalem. The extremists were pre-millennialists and hence
believed that social improvement would come only after the
second coming. Not surprisingly therefore they became increasingly remote from the social activism of the Clapham
moderates.

The 'moderate' Anglican evangelicals tended to be 'dry'
whereas the extremists emphasised emotion, experience and, in
a few cases, prophecy and charismatic gifts. Again, the moderates were not antipathetic to scientific discovery[7] whereas the
Recordites tended to be nervous about accommodating the

beliefs of science. The moderates believed the Bible to be
inspired, but they were not literalists or fundamentalists in the
way that the extremists became in the 1840s.[8]

John Bird Sumner was born into the Clapham moderate
strand of evangelicalism and, despite changes in his views on
many subjects, it can be argued that he remained firmly within
its broader ethos and ideals throughout his life.

A Claphamite Family Circle

John Bird's mother, Hannah Sumner, was the first cousin of
William Wilberforce. Sumner was therefore part of a family
circle which rubbed shoulders with the men and women of
Clapham. Robert, Sumner's father, died when John was com-
pleting his university education and his brother, Charles, was
only fourteen. Hannah sought and received kindly support and
guidance from William Wilberforce.[9] Correspondence shows
that in later years when John had just been consecrated Bishop
of Chester, he endeavoured to return William's kindness by
offering his son a good living in his new diocese.[10] It is note-
worthy that at the time of Sumner's offer, Samuel Wilberforce
had only been a deacon for six months. In the event, it was
John's younger brother, Charles, who repaid William's kindness to the Sumners. He made Samuel Archdeacon of Surrey in
1839 when he was only 34 years of age. Reciprocations between
the Sumners and Wilberforces continued. In later years John
Bird wrote to Samuel who by then had become Bishop of
Oxford thanking him for making his eldest son a welcome guest
at his family's dinner table.[11]

As a young fellow at King's College, Cambridge, John Bird
would inevitably have had frequent contact with Charles Simeon who was part of the Clapham inner circle and gave them
advice on spiritual matters from time to time. It is clear that
Simeon's ideas on preaching and parochial visiting formed the
basis of Sumner's early thinking. A little later in 1820 Sumner
was made a Prebendary of Durham by Bishop Shute Barrington. John Bird's subsequent associations with the Cathedral
strengthened his friendship with a fellow Prebend, Thomas

Gisborne, who held the first stall. Gisborne, the squarson of Yoxhall in Staffordshire, spent time each year working on Clapham projects.[12] When Sumner was consecrated Bishop of Chester in York Minster he chose Gisborne as the preacher for the occasion.[13]

Shortly after his arrival in Chester Sumner appointed Henry Raikes as his Chaplain. Two years later in 1830 Sumner made Raikes Chancellor of the diocese. This drew the favourable comment from Charles Simeon who spoke of the Diocese enjoying the benefits of a sort of double episcopacy.[14] Among other close associates of Sumner were Daniel Wilson (1778–1858), Bishop of Calcutta and Henry Venn (1796–1873), General Secretary of the Church Missionary Society. Sumner shared Daniel Wilson's abhorrence of tractarianism and spoke of him as his 'esteemed friend'. Venn too became a close companion and together they spent many hours discussing the needs and strategies of the colonial Church. Venn was noted by the *Times'* correspondent as one of the chief mourners at Sumner's funeral.[15] During his Chester episcopate some of Sumner's other close associates were also men of moderate evangelical views. These included Archdeacons Hodson and Rushton and Hugh Stowell, incumbent of Christ Church, Manchester. Hodson was an intimate of Charles Simeon[16] and Stowell, according to his biographer, developed 'an intimate friendship which outlasted the mere connection of diocese, and ended only with the death of the venerable archbishop in 1862'.[17]

Patron of Claphamite Societies

Being at home among the moderates of the Clapham school it is no surprise that Sumner became a keen and active supporter of most of the significant broader-based evangelical religious societies. Like many nineteenth-century evangelicals, Sumner was committed to the importance of societies. In his charge of 1832 he declared that such societies 'show an anxious zeal against ungodliness and formal religion.[18] Those societies to which Sumner devoted the bulk of his time were in general those which were founded by the Clapham sect or which had been endorsed by them.

Two of the great societies with Clapham links were the *Church Missionary Society* established in 1799 and the *British and Foreign Bible Society* founded in 1804. The former organisation owed its origin primarily to Charles Simeon, the latter was a specifically Clapham foundation.

In his history of the Church Missionary Society, Eugene Stock gave tribute to the influential support given to the society by John Bird Sumner and his brother Charles, Bishop of Winchester. He wrote: 'These two good men threw themselves heart and soul into the service of the leading religious institutions, and year by year they spoke at meeting after meeting, especially those of the Church Missionary, Jews and Bible Societies.'[19] Sumner was a frequent preacher at CMS Anniversary services. Stock points out that he spoke three times between 1842 and 1849.[20] He also became one of the Society's Vice-Patrons and gave one of the sermons at its Jubilee along with Edward Bickersteth.[21]

Sumner was equally staunch in his support of *The British and Foreign Bible Society* which he joined just two years after it was founded.[22] He was invariably present at the Society's anniversary meetings and was elected a Vice-President in 1848. In 1853 he gave the Jubilee sermon at St Paul's Cathedral, London and spoke eloquently of the society's work over the years.

> Look, however, at the great result. The Bible, in whole or in part, may now be read, not in fifty, but in one-hundred-and-forty-eight languages or dialects; and we may safely calculate that, through the instrumentality of this Society, the Word of God is accessible to six-hundred millions more of the population of the globe than was the case at its establishment fifty years ago. 'Not unto us, O Lord, not unto us, but unto the name be all the praise'.[23]

Even in the year of his death the 82-year-old Primate wrote from Lambeth rejoicing 'at what God has wrought through the society'. In his letter he stated that his 'sentiments respecting the Bible Society are the same which I have held for more than fifty years'. These sentiments, he continued, 'are not likely to change whilst its object and constitution remain the same'.[24]

The Church Pastoral Aid Society and the Lord's Day Observance Society were both institutions which enjoyed the support of the more moderate evangelicals of Clapham sentiments, although the latter was also supported by some 'extremists'. John Bird devoted his energies to them both and was a prime mover in the founding of the CPAS. All the initial plans for the formation of the Society were submitted to him for scrutiny and all the changes which he recommended were accepted by the committee.[25] G.R. Balleine wrote that through the Society's troubled early years 'he was ever ready to defend it on the platform and to give it private advice'.[26] At the first Annual General Meeting it was noted that Sumner guided the Society to 'within the limits by which, as consistent Churchmen, we must be confined'.[27] In 1836 Sumner was listed as one of six vice-Patrons of the Society.[28] In the course of the Annual sermon which he gave in 1838 Sumner spoke of CPAS's vital work. 'They have', he said, 'in the course of two short years, supplied the salaries of 123 curates, and 22 lay assistants; thus doubling the spiritual superintendence of 132 ecclesiastical districts, and of more than a million of the inhabitants of our land'.[29]

The Lord's Day Observance Society, which had been set up in 1831, also drew Sumner's active support. This is hardly surprising given that he had written at length on the uniqueness of the sabbath some fifteen years previously in his Treatise on the Records of Creation. He was therefore heart and soul behind the objectives of the Society, both locally and nationally. For example in February 1834 we find Sumner in the chair at the Chester branch Annual meeting which was held in the Corn Exchange. According to the Chester Chronicle,[30] Sumner spoke of the incalculable blessings arising to man from due observance of the Sabbath. He went on to remark very favourably on the way in which the Sabbath was kept in Chester. 'Passing' through the streets of this city, a few Sabbaths age,' Sumner had 'observed with pleasure the great decorum generally manifested'.[31] Sumner, like the earlier Clapham Sect, was convinced of the importance of achieving Sunday observance by means of government legislation. Unlike them he does not appear to have been motivated by a fear of national judgement in the event of failure. Speaking at the national Annual General Meeting of the Society held at the Exeter Hall on May 1834 Sumner sought to counter those who argued against legislation.[32] People had urged that the poor would be the losers as a result of Parliamentary action. Sumner contended on the contrary that 'the poor man must be the greatest gainer by a measure which would prevent him from being forced to work on the Sabbath'.[33] Despite provoking hostile reaction, Sumner fought throughout his career in support of the legislative measures of the LDOS.[34] He was one of those who prevailed on Lord Palmerston to order the Sunday closure of the National Gallery and the British Museum in 1856. During the same year he also succeeded in stopping Sunday afternoon military band concerts in all London parks.[35] Indeed there seems little doubt that Sumner played a significant role in establishing the Victorian Sunday. For him it was the central aspect of the earlier Clapham movement for the reformation of manners.

In addition to these overtly Claphamite interests, Sumner followed in the groups's footsteps in being a warm supporter of both the *Society for the Propagation of the Gospel* and the *Society for the Promotion of Christian Knowledge*. Although both organisations, became progressively 'high Church' and tractarian in ethos as the nineteenth century progressed, neither was overtly so during Sumner's lifetime. In the earlier part of the century both societies were noted for their good taste, avoidance of controversy and solid attachment to the credal faith. For these reasons Wilberforce and his circle of friends and associates were always ready to support and endorse their activities. Sumner followed suit. During the twenty years of his Chester episcopate, Sumner took the chair at the twice-yearly meetings of the diocesan SPCK on numerous occasions. *The Minute Book of the Chester diocesan SPCK* for example, shows him to have been in the chair on seventeen out of eighteen occasions in the 1830s and 1840s.[36] As Archbishop of Canterbury, Sumner assumed the office of patron of the Society. In March 1849 he preached the Society's Jubilee sermon in St

Paul's Cathedral. The *Illustrated London News* in a feature article on the Jubilee noted that from humble beginnings with only five members the Society had progressed to its present roll of 17,150 members.[37] Charity Schools of which there were now 21,034 originated from the work of SPCK.

One of the original objects of the SPCK had been 'to extend Christian knowledge to the Colonies and Dependencies of the British Empire'. In order to facilitate this, it had established as a separate institution, the *Society for the Propagation of the Gospel in Foreign Parts*, by a royal Charter in 1701. Sumner appears to have given rather less of his time to this Society, but he did nevertheless interest himself in its affairs. While he was at Chester he subscribed on occasion to the Society's District Association.[38] He also preached a sermon on behalf of the Society in Trinity Church[39] in the City in 1834. As Primate Sumner became President of the Society.[40]

Claphamite Pastor and Prelate

If the Societies to which Sumner gave his energies revealed his Clapham coat-tails, his preaching and pastoral work did so even more. As a young Cambridge undergraduate John Bird's commitment to the evangelical faith intensified and deepened under Simeon's ministry. He left University convinced of the supreme importance of good, straightforward well illustrated biblical preaching. Simeon had published his *Horae Homileticae* in 21 volumes and his outlines became the model used by many of the younger generations of clergy who followed him. Sumner was to do likewise and throughout his life he produced practical expositions of most of the books of the New Testament. These were written both for private devotional reading and also to aid busy and over-burdened parish clergy with their Sunday sermons. E.R. Moore commented: 'Sumner's attitudes can thus be seen to mirror those of his mentor, and at the same time prove how fruitful were those labours of Simeon in his rooms at Cambridge.'[41]

As with all evangelicals, Sumner's preaching was crucicentric. Like Simeon he proclaimed the message of Christ and him

crucified. Indeed without a significant reference to the cross in
a sermon Sumner would have felt he had failed his hearers.
Even in a graduation service at Cambridge University in June
1828 Sumner took as his theme bringing the mind of men into
conformity with the mind of God. The means by which this was
achieved, he said, was by means of the cross. Sumner therefore
gave a plain statement of the substitutionary atonement.

> ... the son undertakes the office of reconciliation, He says... Let
> all who trust in me, be forgiven and treated as if they had not
> sinned. Let me be bruised for their transgressions; let me be
> wounded for their iniquities; let the chastisement of their peace
> be laid on me....[42]

Like all evangelicals Sumner preached to the heart. Christianity
was to be experienced in the emotions. 'Be not content with
coldly subscribing to the fact of Christ's cross and passion, as
to an article of faith', he declared on one occasion. He went on
to exhort his hearers 'to feel his mercy in accepting those who
approach him in "the Beloved"'.[43] In his first Charge to the
Diocese of Chester in 1829 Sumner urged upon his brother
clergy the importance of preaching the gospel. 'Wherever an
assemblage of men is collected and located together, he declared, 'provision should be made for their souls'.[44] Such provision meant that 'they be "brought to God" through Christ
Jesus' and 'that they be instructed and maintained in his faith'.[45]
Summarising Sumner spelt to his clerical hearers the crucial
role the atonement plays in the workings of salvation, operating
as it does as the means by which men and women are brought
to God.

> ... the atonement made by the Son of God, the sacrifice of the
> cross is the great instrument of working this conviction.[46]

The Christian Observer later commented that in respect of
preaching Sumner distinguished between 'the legal style' and
'the evangelical style'. It was the latter 'which really awakens
men's hearts, which converts them to God, and enables them to
increase in his Holy Spirit more and more, till they come to his
everlasting Kingdom'.[47]

Another aspect of Sumner's pastoralia which marked him out as an evangelical, was his strong advocacy of district visiting societies and the use of laymen and women to assist in the pastoral care of the parish. Both the Clapham 'moderates' and the more 'extreme' Anglican evangelicals were convinced supporters of lay visitation, but it seems likely given the derivation of so many of his other ideas and principles that Sumner's initial thoughts ideas on this matter came from the Claphamite school. In his first Charge of 1829 Sumner strongly urged incumbents who served the more populous parishes to select men carefully who 'are worthy' and of 'good report'.[48] Such individuals would lessen their own labour 'by visiting and examining the schools, by reading and praying with the infirm and aged, by consoling the fatherless and widows and pursuing the many nameless ways by which it is the power of one Christian to benefit and receive another'.[49] The model Sumner commended was the 'large and populous town of Brighton which has for some years been divided into six districts each of which consists of from nine to eighteen sub-divisions, and has visitors regularly appointed to each subdivision, some males but chiefly females'.[50] One of Brighton's leading clerics for a good part of the nineteenth century was the Revd Henry Venn Elliott (1792–1865). He was the incumbent of St Mary's from 1827 until his death. His uncle, John Venn, was rector of Clapham and he was acquainted with Charles Simeon who on occasion preached to his Brighton congregation. Venn Elliott was a close friend of John Bird Sumner and stayed with him at Addington Park when he was Archbishop of Canterbury.[51]

With the passing of the years Sumner grew in his enthusiasm and commitment to visiting societies. He became a member and keen supporter of the *General Society for Promoting District Visiting*.[52] He was often present at their Annual General Meetings and preached on their behalf.[53]

Moderate on Theological and Social Issues

Sumner also showed himself to be a representative of the Claphamite school in his moderate stance on theological and social issues. In matters biblical, the 'moderates', as Hilton and Bebbington have shown, were less inclined to literalism in their hermeneutic, and were not antipathetic to scientific discovery. The radical Recordite evangelicals tended to proclaim more imminent doctrines of the second coming replete with a historical interpretation of every last apocalyptic detail. In association with this belief, many of them developed elaborate pre-millenarian schemes which were based on detailed understandings of Old Testament prophecy. In contrast, the earlier Simeonite generation of commentators contended that the prophecies of the Old Testament should be read spiritually.

In all these matters Sumner was clearly aligned with the 'moderates'. He believed the Bible to be 'emphatically TRUTH',[54] a source of power in peoples' lives and the instrument of positive change in British society. However, in no sense was Sumner a literalist, or antagonistic to scientific discovery. Although not the first to put forward the view, he was one of the earliest writers to contend that the Genesis account of creation should not be regarded as detailed scientific information. In his *Treatise on the Records of Creation* which was published in 1816 Sumner wrote that 'the account of creation given by Moses, does not prove to furnish anything like a systematic scheme or elaborate detail of the mode in which the materials of the earth were brought to their actual form and situation'.[55] In his writing on the second coming of Christ, Sumner always put the stress not on the suddenness of the event, but on the need for Christian preparedness. Commenting on Jesus' teaching about his second coming in Mark, Chapter 13, Sumner steered away from any speculative notions about dates and times.

> But of that day and hour, either when the judgements of God should fall upon Jerusalem, or when mankind should be summoned to their great account, God will not see fit to make precise revelation.[56]

Sumner went on to stress the need for Christian people to be in constant readiness. 'We are assured' he wrote 'that it will happen. And to be prepared whenever it happens, this is the trial of faith.'[57] He made a more or less similar point in his exposition of the second letter of Peter Chapter three. Commenting on the new heavens and the new earth Sumner wrote: 'This much God has clearly revealed. The season when it shall take place he has not disclosed.'[58] His understanding of the events of the early chapters of Genesis also avoided rigid literalism.

Sumner was criticised by some for admitting that 'the Bible is not infallible'[59] and for taking a 'moderate' approach to certain hermeneutical techniques. However his opinions were stoutly defended by others, the *Christian Observer* commenting that the well-informed Christian public will not be disposed to set down such men as opposers of the Bible and allies of infidelity'.[60]

In his doctrine and teaching Sumner deliberately avoided extremes and excesses. Like the Claphamites he inclined to post-millenarian ideas. There is no evidence to suggest that he ever showed any interest in charismatic phenomena or the spiritual gifts which were so closely associated with the pre-millenial school. He retained to the end of his days the moderate, reasoned but spiritual opinions which he had embraced as a young man. Indeed, his death and that of his younger brother Charles in 1874 might perhaps be regarded as marking the effectual passing of the nineteenth-century Clapham moderate school of Anglican evangelicalism.

Notes

1. See Bebbington D., *Evangelicalism in Modern Britain* (Unwin Hyman, 1989), p. 1.
2. See Bebbington D., *ibid.*, pp. 1–19; Hilton B., *The Age of the Atonement* (Clarendon, 1988), pp. 3–35.
3. Bebbington D., *op. cit.*, pp. 2–17.
4. Hilton B., *op. cit.*, pp. 8–29.
5. *Ibid.*, pp. 10, 11.
6. *Ibid.*, p. 10, 11.
7. *Ibid.*, pp. 22.
8. Bebbington D., *op. cit.*, pp. 88–90.
9. See for example Hannah Sumner to Wilberforce 30 June 1812 (MS C3 fol. 127, Bodleian Library, Oxford).

10. See for example William Wilberforce Correspondence (MS C3 fol. 215, Bodleian Library, Oxford).

11. Ashwell A.R., *Life of Samuel Wilberforce* (John Murray, 1881), Vol. 1, p. 436.

12. See Stephen Sir James, *Essays in Ecclesiastical Biography* (Longman, Green, Reader and Dyer, 1875), p. 535.

13. The *Record*, 19 September 1828.

14. Moore E.R., *John Bird Sumner Bishop of Chester 1828–48* (unpublished MA thesis, University of Manchester, 1976), p. 48.

15. *Times* (London), 10 September 1862

16. See Carus W., *Memoirs of the Life of the Revd. Charles Simeon MA*, (London, Hatchard & Son, 1848), pp. 553–554.

17. Marsden J.B., *Memoirs of the Life and Labours of the Rev. Hugh Stowell MA* (London, Hamilton Adams & Co., 1868), p. 38.

18. Sumner J.B. *A Charge delivered to Clergy of the Diocese of Chester 1832* (J. Hatchard, 1832), p. 22.

19. Stock E., *History of the Church Missionary Society* (CMS, 1899), Vol. 1, p. 258.

20. *Ibid.*, p. 258.

21. *Ibid.*, Vol. 1, p. 492. See also Birks T.R., *A Memoir of Edward Bickersteth* (John Murray, 1863), Vol. 2, p. 408.

22. *Christian Observer* 31 May 1848.

23. Sumner J.B., *A Sermon preached at the Metropolitan Cathedral of St Paul on the Occasion of the Jubilee of the British and Foreign Bible Society on Wednesday March 9, 1853* (Seeleys, 1853), p. 16.

24. The *Record*, 9 May 1862.

25. Balleine G.R., *History of the Evangelical Party in the Church of England* (Longman Green & Co., 1933), p.196.

26. *Ibid.*, p. 196.

27. Report on the First Annual General Meeting of the Church Pastoral Aid Society, *Christian Observer*, October 1836.

28. *Ibid.*

29. *Report of the Third Annual General Meeting of the Church Pastoral Aid Society* (London, J. Hatchard, 1838), p. 16.

30. *Chester Chronicle*, 21 February 1834.

31. *Ibid.*

32. The *Record*, 5 May 1834.

33. *Ibid.*
34. Bradley I., *The Call to Seriousness* (Jonathan Cape, 1976), p. 105.
35. *Ibid.*, p. 105.
36. *Minute Book of the Chester Diocesan SPCK* MS EDD1/18 (Chester County Archives).
37. *The Illustrated London News*, 10 March 1849.
38. See for example *Chester District Association for the Society for the Propagation of the Gospel 1831–1881* MS ED1/19 (Chester County Archives).
39. *Ibid.*
40. See *Crockford's Clerical Directory* 1860 entry for J.B. Sumner.
41. Moore E.R., *op. cit.*, p. 67.
42. Sumner J.B., *A Sermon Preached at St Mary's Church Cambridge on Commencement, Sunday 29 June*, 1828, p. 6.
43. *Ibid.*, p. 12.
44. Sumner J.B., *A Charge Delivered to the Clergy of the Diocese of Chester at the Primary Visitation in August and September 1829* (London, J. Hatchard, 1829), p. 3.
45. *Ibid.*, p. 3.
46. *Ibid.*, p. 9.
47. *Christian Observer*, January 1830.
48. Sumner J.B., *op. cit.*, p. 22.
49. *Ibid.*, p. 23.
50. *Ibid.*, p. 32.
51. Bateman J., *The Life of the Rev. Henry Venn Elliott* (OUP, 1938 edn.), p. 238.
52. See for example *The Fourth Annual Report of the General Society for Promoting Christian Visiting* (British Museum MS 4765 AF21).
53. The *Record* 29 April 1833.
54. Sumner J.B., *A Sermon on the Occasion of the Jubilee of the British and Foreign Bible Society* (Seeleys, 1853), Bodleian Library MS 84 A2618, p. 9.
55. Sumner J.B., *Treatise on the Record of Creation* (1816), p. 270.
56. Sumner J.B., *A Practical Exposition of the Gospels of St Matthew and St Mark* (London, J. Hatchard & Son, 1834), p. 589.
57. *Ibid.*, p. 589.

58. Sumner J.B., *A Practical Exposition of the General Epistles of James, Peter, John and Jude* (London, J. Hatchard & Son, 1840), p. 274.

59. *Ibid.*, p. 194.

60. *Christian Observer*, February 1828.

8

Primate of All England

Elevation to the Primacy

Archbishop Howley died in February 1848 in the middle of a crisis over proposals to consecrate Renn Hampden as Bishop of Hereford. Ten years previously there had been an outcry at Hampden's being made Regius Professor of Divinity in the University of Oxford.[1] Serious questions had been raised as to his orthodoxy on matters relating to his Christological and Trinitarian beliefs. Particularly vigorous protests had come from Newman and the tractarians strongly backed by Samuel Wilberforce[2] who became Bishop of Oxford in 1845.

In the winter of 1847 when Lord John Russell announced the appointment of Hampden there was an immediate outcry from the bench of bishops. Samuel Wilberforce organised a remonstrance which questioned the expediency of the appointment. It was signed by thirteen bishops. Taking into account that two sees were vacant, it amounted to a majority of the existing bishops. Sumner was one of the few who refused to sign. He did so for two reasons. First, he felt that whilst there had been earlier doubts about Hampden's orthodoxy no questions had been raised during his ten years of office in the University. Secondly, he felt that if the appointment had been offered, it was too late to rescind it. On 26 November he penned a letter to C.T. Longley, Bishop of Ripon, in which he spoke positively of Hampden's recent years.

> I remember Dr Hampden's magnificent lecture, which was, and was generally allowed to be, sound divinity. I have occasionally

read some of his .sermons since published, and record the
general impression that they are highly satisfactory; and had
consequently acquiesced in the idea that the error of his Bamp-
ton Lectures were rather errors of expression, than of heretical
theology.[3]

Sumner went on to inform Longley that he had read some of
Hampden's recent lectures fairly closely and 'I cannot find in
them the sentiments which the Bishop of Oxford imputes to Dr
H.'[4] In fact Sumner found quite the reverse. 'The Sixth lecture',
he declared, 'could not have been written by one who had an
erroneous view of the great doctrines of the Gospel'.[5] For these
reasons, and for the fact that 'if the bishopric has been actually
offered it can hardly be withdrawn'. Sumner declined to 'set
my name to the Memorial'.[6] In a letter dated the following day
addressed to Samuel Wilberforce, Sumner wrote: 'Dr H. has
been lecturing and publishing for 12 years since the sentence
was passed against him, the courts were open when he might
have been indicted.[7] Rather than judge Hampden on his Bamp-
ton lecture of ten years earlier John Bird 'thought it more
charitable to form my opinion from the subsequent writings,
especially the conclusion of the pamphlet on the Thirty-Nine
Articles'.[8]

As things stood, it would have been difficult for Lord John
Russell to translate any of those bishops to Canterbury who had
expressed opposition to appointment of Hampden. His choice
therefore fell on Sumner, a move which delighted both Queen
Victoria and her husband Prince Albert.[9] Samuel Wilberforce
wrote regretfully: 'I am very glad it is Chester, not the others.
Now about myself: I feel if it had not been for the Hampden
controversy I should very probably have been put there.'[10]

Sumner's elevation to the primacy was confirmed according
to the custom in Bow Church in March 1848. Opposition had
been expected from some of the tractarians who rejected Sumner's protestant views on baptism and justification.[11] In the
event matters passed off without any untoward occurrence and
John Bird was enthroned in person in Canterbury Cathedral on
28 April.[12] He was supported by the Bishop of Lichfield and his
brother, the Bishop of Winchester. Both *The Times* and the

Record in their accounts of the day's proceedings noted the presence of the Marquis and Marchioness of Conyngham together with Lord Albert Conyngham.[13] Henry Wilberforce returned home from the day's proceedings amused at the spectacle of the evangelical archbishop's submission to the elaborate ritual. 'It was', he wrote, 'important as a precedent to have J.B. walk in procession chanting the psalms from the Chapter nave through the cloisters... then up the nave into the Choir'. All the while outside there stood a man with a great placard which announced: 'Ridiculous Farce—carrying the Pope in Procession'. 'Only think of poor Chester', Wilberforce continued, 'after 68 or 69 years turning into the Pope!'[14]

Sumner's appointment was widely welcomed. His brother Charles wrote:

> It is quite remarkable how universal consent has been given to my brother's appointment. Of course I am not well placed to judge this, and I do not speak from what is said to me, but I hear of satisfaction from all quarters, high and low... I cannot say how thankfully I look forward to closer and nearer intercourse with him.[15]

The *Illustrated London News* commented that he had been raised 'not by political party—nor by the favour of court influence—nor by the recommendation of his Episcopal brethren—but on account of his talents and character alone'.[16] The *Record* greeted Sumner's appointment in terms of unbridled enthusiasm.[17]

Significantly one of John Bird's first episcopal acts as Primate, even before his enthronement, was the consecration of Renn Hampden to the see of Hereford.[18]

The Key Issues of Sumner's Primacy

The measured approach displayed by John Bird Sumner over the Hampden affair was to prove a vital quality during the years of his primacy. His fourteen years in office were beset by theological controversy and ecclesiastical disputes. Among the sensitive issues were the rising tide of ritualism, the Gorham

affair, the revival of the Convocations and the disputes concerning *Essays and Reviews*.

The Rising Tide of Ritualism

The first phase of the Oxford movement which ended with the
publication of Newman's tract 90 in 1841 was largely concerned with doctrinal issues. There was little visible change in
the ornamentation of tractarian churches or in the ceremonial
of their worship. However, in the second phase which emerged
in the later 1840s following Newman's reception into the
Roman Catholic Church, things began to change. Edward
Pusey and other members of the inner circle of leaders deliberately sought to recover and incorporate the practices of the
undivided Catholic Church of the first four centuries into the
life of the Church of England. This resulted in the re-introduc-
tion of a number of the beliefs and practices of the medieval
church for the first time since the Reformation. Set against the
background of rising Roman Catholic influence prompted by
high Irish immigration and the restoration of the Roman Catholic hierarchy in 1851, a widespread outcry ensued. The years of
Sumner's primacy witnessed some of the severest ritualistic
struggles of the century. The situation demanded of him the
utmost wisdom and tact.

One of the first ritualists with whom Sumner had to contend
was the Revd William Dodsworth. Amongst other complaints
which had been raised against him were his advocacy of stone
altars and prayers for the dead. Even Lord John Russell was
sufficiently stirred to write to Sumner on the matter. Sumner's
response was judicious. A stone altar could receive condemnation in the courts because it was opposed to the letter of the
rubric. A condemnation of prayers for the dead would not
because 'the articles were silent on that subject'.[19]

Another issue which came to the fore early in Sumner's
period of office was the question of vestments. A group of
Plymouth clergy wrote complaining about the introduction of
these 'obsolete forms' which 'appear to savour of Romish
superstition'. Once again Sumner showed restraint. Although
he disapproved of wearing Roman eucharistic robes he replied

that a 'season of excitement is not a season for reasonable deliberation'. He also made it clear that 'it is difficult to interfere in the affairs of another diocese'.[20]

The year 1851 produced a correspondence published in *The Times* between Sumner and William Maskell, incumbent of St Mary's Church Torquay. Maskell was an advanced ritualist who announced his intention to secede to the Church of Rome following the decision of the Judicial Committee of the Privy Council in favour of Gorham. Maskell was evidently popular with his parishioners who wrote on his behalf to Sumner requesting that he would not accept their vicar's resignation. In a last attempt to try and assure himself that his position was tenable, Maskell wrote to Sumner setting out his own views. These included the belief that baptism conveyed regeneration, that the Holy Spirit is given in a sacramental manner through the bishop's hands in confirmation, and that episcopacy is the essence of the Church. Sumner replied from Lambeth disclaiming 'all right to answer authoritatively'.[21] He nevertheless did not 'refuse to state, though very briefly, the few remarks which occur to me'.[22] Sumner's letter was cautious being confined entirely to the wording of the Articles and Prayer Book together with the teaching of scripture. Commenting for example on Maskell's statement that episcopacy is of the essence of the Church, Sumner replied: 'Our Church is satisfied with saying that "from the apostles' time there have been three orders, bishops, priests and deacons".'[23] Equally, responding to Maskell's contention that justification is always concurrent with the due reception of the sacrament of baptism'. Sumner wrote: 'The Church can only speak as the scripture speaks... "we are accounted righteous before God, only for the merit of our Lord and Saviour Jesus Christ by faith".' In a second exchange of letters Maskell asked Sumner could he teach these doctrines? Sumner replied 'Are they in the word of God?'[24]

In the autumn of the same year another pastoral exchange took place. This time it was between Sumner and a certain W.R. Gawthorn. Gawthorne wrote to Sumner under the false name of W. Francis. Although in reality a papist, he declared himself to be a protestant. He asked the archbishop for his view on the

question of the invalidity of non-episcopal ordination. Gawthorne claimed that the Archbishop's response would help him
to sort out his own faith. Sumner replied that he hardly imagined
'that there are two bishops on the bench or one clergyman in
fifty throughout our Church who would deny the validity of the
orders of these clergy solely on account of their wanting the
imposition of episcopal hands. Gawthorne had thus by covert
means demonstrated that Sumner did not regard episcopal
ordination as the essential guarantee of the validity of orders.
Sumner's position that episcopacy is of the *bene esse* of the
Church rather than of the *plene esse* angered many high churchman but was declared by the *Christian Observer* to be 'the
genuine doctrine of the Church of England'.[25]

One of the problems which faced the ecclesiastical hierarchy
in all of this was the imprecise nature of the law. Sumner wrote
to Russell that 'the bishops are decidedly opposed to the imita-
tions of Romish customs which have been introduced within
some churches.... If more effectual measures have not been
taken, this is not owing to any approval of these novel usages
on the part of the bishops, but to the uncertainty attending the
state of the law.'[26]

In the summer of 1853 a more vehement outcry resulted from
a series of three sermons preached in Wells Cathedral by George
Denison, Vicar of East Brent and Archdeacon of Taunton.
Backed by the Evangelical Alliance, Joseph Ditcher, the incumbent of the adjoining parish, laid a formal complaint to Archbishop Sumner. Initially Sumner referred the matter back to the
Bishop of Bath and Wells. However when it was found that the
bishop was patron of the living of East Brent, matters were
referred back to Sumner who appointed a commission. Sumner
then held court at Bath on 25 July 1855 with Dr Lushington as
his assessor. Lushington maintained that certain passages taken
from the sermons were contrary to the teaching of the Church
of England. Denison refused to retract and was in consequence
deprived of all his preferments. Among Denison's teaching, the
following were condemned. First that the body and blood of
Christ were really present after an immaterial and spiritual
manner in the consecrated bread and wine and are received by

all who partake in communion. Second, that worship is due to the *real* though invisible presence of the body and blood of Christ.

The decision against Denison created an immediate crisis. The Gorham judgement had made it impossible for high churchmen to turn evangelicals out of the Church of England. Denison's condemnation made it possible for evangelicals to turn out high churchmen. Eventually it emerged that the suit against Denison had not been commenced within the time required by the *Church Discipline Act* and the charge was reversed. A number of high churchmen, including William Gladstone, were nevertheless deeply hurt over the matter, but the *Christian Observer* commended 'the learned, laborious and unprejudiced Judgement of the Archbishop'.[27]

Sumner devoted part of his Canterbury diocesan charge of 1853 to questions raised by the ritualists. He spoke of those who 'have gone to Rome... because of a belief that sin after baptism needs confession, absolution and the sacrament'.[28] Sumner argued that if Confession and absolution were regular practice in the early Church there would at the very least have been mention of the fact in the New Testament epistles.[29] He went on to speak of those who had left the Church of England for this reason as 'victims of delusion'. They have forsaken the 'fountain of living waters', and drunk of 'unsalutary streams'.[30]

In May 1858 the Bishop of London, Campbell Tait, withdrew the licence of William Poole, Curate of St Barnabas Pimlico, following an accusation over his hearing of confession. Sarah Buckingham had been involved in prostitution and it was alleged that Poole had compromised himself in the darkened vestry by asking improper questions. Poole appealed to the Archbishop of Canterbury who without hearing him confirmed the Bishop of London's action in July 1858. Poole went to the secular court who required Sumner to hear the appeal. In March 1859 Sumner heard the appeal and declared that 'the proved and admitted allegations afford, in the language of the statute, good and reasonable cause for the revocation of his licence'.[31] Sumner went on to state that the course pursued by Poole was not only 'not in accordance with the rubric or doctrine of the

Church of England, but most dangerous, and likely to cause
serious mischief to the cause of morality and religion'.[32]

The controversy between the ritualists and the Church authorities reached a high point shortly after the Poole judgement.
Queen Victoria herself addressed a letter to Sumner requiring
him as Primate of all England 'to take such measures, agreeable
to both the laws of our realm and the rights of our Royal
Prerogative... as shall seem to you best fitted to repress any such
disorders and innovations'. The Queen spoke of these innovations as 'those corruptions' from which 'the Church was by the
blessing of God mercifully delivered at the period of the Reformation'.[33] She charged Sumner to ensure that those instructions were carried out by all diocesan bishops. Whatever may
be said of Sumner's dealings with the ritualists, it is clear that
he did his best to carry out the Queen's instructions in a firm
but fairminded manner.

The Gorham Affair

Possibly the greatest controversy of Sumner's primacy was
provoked by Tractarian and High Church teaching on infant
baptism. This teaching was at the centre of what came to be
known as the Gorham affair. Thomas Dampier, Bishop of Ely,
raised questions about George Cornelius Gorham's[34] understanding of baptismal regeneration, but eventually consented to
his ordination in 1811. Gorham was elected a fellow of his
College in the same year and remained in office until his
marriage in 1827. He then served several curacies including
Clapham, before Lord Lyndhurst presented him with the valuable living of St Just-in-Penwyth, Cornwall.

In November 1847 Lord Chancellor Cottenham presented
him with the less demanding parish of Brampford Speke near
Exeter. Bishop Phillpotts, whose hackles had already been
aroused by Gorham having advertised the previous year for a
curate 'free of tractarian error', first demanded to examine him
on the matter of baptismal regeneration. This took place on 17,
18, 21 and 22 December 1847 and later on 10 March 1848. The
examination brought the Church of England's teaching on
baptismal regeneration into public view. High churchmen such

as Phillpotts and ritualists asserted that the baptised infant was regenerate. Evangelicals maintained that such regeneration was conditional on the subsequent faith of the child. George Gorham's views were strongly Calvinist and although they did not exactly fit with either party, they were nonetheless quite close to those of some less moderate evangelicals. He contended that regeneration might be given before baptism or subsequently.

Bishop Phillpotts based his arguments largely on the language of the Prayer Book services while Gorham took his stand on the Articles of Religion. Phillpotts found Gorham an able theologian, but nevertheless refused to institute him. After losing his case in the Court of Arches, Gorham appealed to the judicial committee of the Privy Council, which reversed the decision in his favour. Sumner was one of the judges appointed by the Privy Council which gave judgement that 'Mr Gorham had not taught doctrine contrary to the teaching of the Church of England'.[35] Numbers of laity and clergy were doubtful about the composition and the decision of the council, but Sumner was quick to defend both. He wrote to Bishop Samuel Wilberforce: 'I feel bound to bear witness to the patient investigation which the question received, and the earnest of the members of the committee to pronounce such a sentence as should be in accordance, both in letter and spirit, with our Articles and formularies.'[36] The Bishop of Exeter's response was to issue a public pronouncement excommunicating Sumner and any who would seek on his behalf to institute Gorham to the living of Brampford Speke. In what was a major public controversy Sumner showed dignity and forbearance. He did what had to be done in the circumstances and gave authority to the Dean of Arches to institute Gorham on 6 August 1850. He acted in a firm, but gracious spirit. The majority of churchmen were of the opinion that justice had been done and that the practice of the Church in the matter of baptism since the Reformation had been upheld.

The Revival of Convocation

Many tractarians and high churchmen were deeply disturbed by the Gorham controversy, as much by the part that the final tribunal of appeal in a doctrinal dispute had been a secular not ecclesiastical court, as by the upholding of Gorham's views. As they saw it, the Church was a divine society, the body of Christ, and its affairs, particularly those concerning the faith, should never be allowed to fall under the judgement of a secular authority. The situation led to calls for the revival of convocation, the Church's Parliament which consisted of bishops and representatives of the clergy. In the sixteenth-century Reformation settlement the monarch had become the Supreme Governor of the Church of England, but the Convocation still existed and in the view of many high Churchmen had the right to determine matters of doctrine. In practice whilst Convocations did meet, they did so only as a matter of form. They could not transact any business unless summoned to do so by the monarch. No King or Queen had summoned either Convocation to business since 1717.[37]

Matters came to a head in 1851 when Lord Redesdale took the opportunity of introducing a bill into the House of Lords to revive Convocation. The bill was supported by Charles Blomfield, the Bishop of London, and Samuel Wilberforce, the Bishop of Oxford. Sumner however opposed it on the grounds that it would be a source of much controversy. In his speech during the debate in the Lords, Sumner gave two reasons for opposing the revival of Convocations. First, the nature of the business to be discussed was too controversial. Secondly, Sumner argued that the liturgy and doctrine had been formulated by Parliament, not by Convocation. Convocation therefore had no right to debate these matters. In this he shared the views of Lord John Russell who regarded the revival of Convocation as to 'put in hazard the Queen's Supremacy over all matters in the Church, spiritual as well as temporal, and revive those fierce disputes which at the beginning of the last century made the meetings of Convocation a scandal and a public nuisance'.[38]

When the Convocation of Canterbury met in February 1851 Samuel Wilberforce presented a petition supported by the Bish-

ops of London, Exeter and Chichester urging that some business might be discussed. The Queen's Advocate declared this
suggestion to be illegal on the ground that Henry VIII's *Statute
25,C19* prohibited Convocation doing any business without the
express sanction of the crown. Sumner therefore prorogued the
meeting on the ground that it was most improper that Convocation should place itself in hostility to the government.[39]

However, later in the same month, Russell's government
resigned following a Commons defeat. Lord Derby who came
to office thought differently and advised the Crown to issue
licences to allow Convocation to discuss business. Sumner still
felt strongly about such proposals and spoke out against them
in his charge of 1853. 'The revival of Convocations', he declared, 'would not tend to promote the great interests of our
ministry, the establishment of personal religion amongst our
people, or the advancement of religion generally throughout the
land'. 'Our duty', he maintained, was 'to seek for Christ's
sheep... who are in the midst of this naughty world, that they
may be saved through Christ'.[40] Several further attempts were
made to revive the Convocations, but it was not until Lord
Aberdeen's government met in February 1854 that it was finally
agreed that appropriate business could be considered. In July
1854 Sumner wrote to Lord Aberdeen as follows:

> The assembling of Parliament is accompanied with the sum-
> mons to convocation. This used to be reckoned and treated as
> mere form, except at the meeting of a new Parliament. But an
> effort will certainly be made to proceed to business.[41]

Sumner went on to ask Lord Aberdeen for an audience 'that I
should be made acquainted with your Lordship's wishes and
intentions concerning this'.[42]

Although such moves were against Sumner's better judgement, he nevertheless showed himself magnanimous. He
willingly accepted the Lower House of Convocation's own
nomination of prolocutor when he had the power to make his
own appointment. He even wrote to Lord Aberdeen stating that
he felt it appropriate to allow Convocation to continue 'for one
perhaps two days beyond the day of meeting on Tuesday 6
February'.[43] In a subsequent interchange of letters, Lord Aberdeen

replied that 'knowing the opinions of Your Grace on the subject of Convocation and relying on the discretion and moderation of your views, I am content to leave the matter in Your Grace's hands'.[44]

As things turned out the revival of Convocation did not provoke the time of crisis which Sumner had anticipated. Certainly there was during his prelature no attempt to revise the Prayer Book or to move the Church of England in a Romeward direction. A study of the *Chronicle of Convocation* reveals that although Sumner chaired the debates of the Upper house he very rarely spoke or made comments on the motions under debate.[45]

Although Sumner might be thought reactionary in his stance over Convocations, he nevertheless displayed the capacity to be flexible once the decision to revive their active role in the Church had been taken.

Essays and Reviews

In 1861, the year before Sumner died, another major crisis confronted the Church of England with the publication of a collection of writings under the title *Essays and Reviews*.[46] The volume which was edited by Henry Wilson, a country cleric and former Oxford fellow, had seven contributors all of whom were Anglicans, six of them ordained. Each aimed to take note of the findings of critical biblical scholarship and recent discoveries in science particularly in the realm of geology. The individual contributions varied in style and content and in the degree to which they were felt to be offensive by both the Church and the wider public. Two contributors, Henry Wilson (1803–88) and Benjamin Jowett, (1817–93), were prosecuted in the Church courts and suspended from office for a period of twelve months. Wilson wrote on the inspiration of scripture and contended that the Church of England Articles nowhere claimed the Bible to be 'inspired'.[47] Jowett maintained that scripture 'is like any other book' and had but one meaning namely that which was intended by the biblical writer to his original readers.[48] Other essayists asserted that Genesis chapter one could not be regarded as scientific, that Moses did not write the Pentateuch, that the suffering servant of Isaiah chapter 53 did not refer to Jesus and that Daniel could not be regarded as an historical person.[49]

Understandably there was a widespread outcry against the publication from all quarters. In particular both high Churchmen and evangelicals were on the offensive. The *Record* for example denounced the essayists as 'Septem Contra Christum'.[50] The *Christian Observer* commented cynically that the present volume was meant to establish the principle that a man may retain the orders and benefices of the Church without believing the Bible'.[51]

By February 1861 addresses and protests of one kind or another were flowing steadily towards the bishops. Sumner convened the bench at Lambeth and they decided to make a public reply to one of them. The particular address which they answered came from a Dorsetshire rural deanery. They wished 'to make known to your grace and to all the bishops the alarm we feel at the late indications of the spread of rationalistic and semi-infidel doctrines among the beneficed clergy'.[52] Sumner replied from Lambeth in a letter dated 12 February 1861 that he and his brother bishops 'cannot understand how these opinions can be held consistently with an honest subscription to the formularies of our Church'. He concluded by pointing out that the solution was that 'we and the clergy of our several dioceses may be enabled to preach that good deposit of sound doctrine which our Church teaches in its fullness.'[53]

Following this pronouncement, Bishop Walter Kerr Hamilton (1808–69), the saintly Tractarian diocesan Bishop of Salisbury, instigated proceedings against one of the essayists, Rowland Williams (1817–1870) in the Court of Arches in June 1861. Williams, who was Professor of Hebrew and Vice-Principal of St David's College Lampeter, also held the small Wiltshire living of Broadchalke. He thus came under Hamilton's jurisdiction. The prosecution was something of a risky undertaking because if he had lost he would have been required to find costs from his own pocket. For this reason Sumner and his brother Charles offered financial aid. In the event Williams was condemned and suspended from his benefice for one year.[54]

The Church Estates

The period of Sumner's primacy was one in which there was much debate about the care and management of Church property. The *Ecclesiastical Commission*, which had been established under Sir Robert Peel in 1836, continued throughout Sumner's Archiepiscopacy to try and improve the Church's structure and finances. In November 1848 Lord John Russell suggested to Sumner that three persons be appointed to the Commission with the specific role of 'making the property of the Church more valuable'.[55] The act which eventually emerged in 1850 from these proposals made provision for Church lands to be administered by the three estates commissioners appointed by government supported by two members, one a layman appointed by the Ecclesiastical Commission. A quorum of three had executive power provided that two of the three were estates commissioners. Sumner was against these proposals because it removed the real control from the bishops. He wrote from Addington to Lord John Russell on 14 January that 'I forsee decided opposition to the proposed scheme on the part of many colleagues who will complain of... having their estates taken out of their own hands'.[56] In general it can be said that in an age in which successive governments sought to lay hands on Church title and property, Sumner fought hard to maintain the interests of the Church where the Church's position was tenable. For example, he was very critical of the increased rent charges to clergy which the government proposed in its *Tithes Assessment and Rent Charges Bill*. He also strongly opposed the provision of the *Episcopal and Capitular Estates Management Bill* which aimed to give to tenants permanent rights to rent Church lands.[57] Even on the matter of Church rates which Lord John Russell urged should be thrown 'entirely upon the voluntary contributions of their congregation',[58] Sumner was of the view that some form of obligatory payment should continue.[59]

Canterbury Diocese

Alongside these national issues, not to mention his widespread concern for the Colonial Church (see separate chapter), Sumner also administered the Canterbury Diocese with the same dedicated spiritual devotion which characterised all his labours.[60] In his new capacity as Bishop of the Diocese John Bird concerned himself most prominently with the issues of education, Church buildings and the role of his clergy as communicators of the Christian message.

His years in Chester had convinced Sumner of the paramount importance of education and the building of schools. He began his first Charge to the Diocese in 1849 by raising the question of the management of schools. 'I cannot refrain from expressing my own conviction', he said 'that, practically, the government of the school will be in the hands of the Clergyman'.[61] As Sumner saw it, if the clergyman failed in this duty, others would take it upon themselves and Christian influence might be irrecoverably lost. In his own words: 'The literary character of the school will depend upon its master; but the religious character of the school most depends upon the clergyman.'[62] Although the *Canterbury National Schools' Minute Book* indicates that he rarely attended meetings, Sumner was quick to appreciate the great value of their work. In his charge of 1853 he congratulated them on the establishment of a system of Diocesan inspection which had already furnished reports on 406 in the diocese.[63] Sumner was able to comment with satisfaction that 'few places remain where there is no access to a National School'.[64]

In contrast to his former Diocese, Canterbury did not share the same widespread need for more Church buildings and increased accommodation. Nevertheless some areas such as Croydon, Maidstone, Folkestone and Dover were experiencing rapid population growth. In the last census to have been taken prior to Sumner's coming to office, Croydon was reported to have exceeded 20,000 inhabitants while the parish church and chapels could afford sittings for only 4,200 persons of which only 493 were free.[65] Sumner recognised that more new churches and Chapels were needed. In addition many existing buildings 'had suffered from the effects of time.'[66]

During his Canterbury episcopate Sumner consecrated 30 new Churches with sittings for 11,000, 7,000 of which were free.[67] In addition he consecrated four major restorations and one replacement Church building. Addressing his Clergy in 1857 he spoke of his comfort that 'in my present Diocese the accommodation provided in the Churches is, with few exceptions, equal to the demand'.[68]

In all of this Sumner was quick to recognise the major role played by the *Incorporated Society*. This body had during the last thirty years 'aided either the building or the enlarging of eighty-four of our Churches'.[69]

Throughout his life Sumner clung steadfastly to the belief that the lack of Church buildings and adequate seating was a major reason why so many remained 'outside the pale of our Church'.[70] He seemed not to appreciate that many new Church buildings were cold, unwelcoming and made the poor feel at the very least out of place or second-class citizens. However, Sumner was ever ready to remind the Clergy that their role was a crucial one, and that how they received new adherents was central to the process of these new Christians becoming part of the Church.

In his Charge of 1849 Sumner devoted the bulk of his attention to the duties of the Clergyman. These he saw in terms of being a Watchman and a Steward. Here Sumner's plain evangelical faith surfaces in eloquent tones. The Watchman's duty, he declares, is to:

> ... lay before the people the divine will as regards mankind: the total ruin in which they are involved through the sin of our first parents; the only mode of restoration through the reliance on the atonement made for them on the Cross: and the sole proof of an interest in that atonement, a holy and obedient life.[71]

Sumner urged that this message be proclaimed with unmistakeable black-and-whiteness.[72] He urged his Clergy not to read sermons but to learn the art of 'conversation preaching'. 'Congregations', he said, 'are to be discoursed with, not read to'. Sumner supported the wishes of his predecessor and stressed the need for two sermons on Sunday. In his view in a day when many could not read, or read only very little, two sermons were essential.

Throughout his life Sumner had taken a keen interest in the education and training of the Clergy. During his time in Chester he had encouraged the work of the theological Colleges at St Bees and at Birkenhead. On his arrival at Canterbury one of his first duties was to consecrate the chapel and buildings of the new St Augustine's College. The project had arisen in response to the pleas for a steady supply of trained clergy which came from James Broughton, the first bishop sent to Australia. The founders of St Augustine's, Beresford Hope and Edward Coleridge, had a decided vision for 'a Catholic not a protestant seminary'.[73] In earlier years Sumner had spoken strongly against the concept of such a partisan high-Church college training clergy for the Colonial Church and had declined to become one of the institution's Vice-presidents. Now however as the newly consecrated Archbishop of Canterbury he found himself 'perpetual visitor' by virtue of the College Charter. Sumner showed himself to be gracious and magnanimous. He performed the consecration, preached the sermon based on Ephesians chapter 3 verse 10 and presided at the Communion service, which was attended by John Keble and others with a decidedly high-church view of mission. Despite his personal misgivings Sumner continued to give what support he could to the College and in 1857 he sanctioned the granting of a College diploma.

Despite his age, during this period Sumner remained in vigorous health. In 1857 he publicly gave thanks that 'there was little sign of that abatement of health and strength which my advancing years would give me just reason to expect'.[74] Even in his very last years his energy and workload were more akin to a man of sixty than an octogenarian! He continued to travel throughout the Diocese right up until the month before he died. His last act was to consecrate the new Church of St James the Apostle, Dover on 20 August 1862. He died on 6 September in Addington.

Although he was an able academic, a competent administrator, a lucid writer and a gifted preacher whose sonorous voice and easy manner was eagerly sought after, he was remembered by all, and particularly those in his own diocese, as a saintly dignified man whose simple lifestyle and gracious manner commended him to everyone of whatever party or station in life.[75] R.C. Jenkins in his history of Canterbury diocese wrote of Sumner having 'left an image never to be effaced in the memory of all who witnessed it.'[76] Jenkins paid this tribute to Sumner's work in the diocese.

> Few will fail to remember the energy and devotion with which up to the very last the archbishop entered upon all the duties which the care of the diocese devolved upon him. Up to his latest years he carried on his progress in the diocese, every part of which was known personally to him; and when he was urged to intermit in some degree this active oversight, he was accustomed to say that the time would come when he might be unequal to it, but till then he was anxious to continue his personal knowledge of his diocese. Travelling in the simplest manner with a single servant, and only distinguished by that graceful dignity which was ever conspicuous in him, he is remembered everywhere as realising that ideal of Apostolic ministry which he had traced in his earliest and most popular work.[77]

Notes

1. For the crisis surrounding Hampden's appointment as Professor of Divinity in the University of Oxford, see Chadwick O., *The Victorian Church* (A. & C. Black, 1970), pp. 112–26.

2. See Ashwell A.R., *The Life of the Right Reverend Samuel Wilberforce* (John Murray, 1880), Vol. 1, pp. 434–437.

3. Sumner J.B. to Longley C.T., 26 November 1847, *Longley Papers*, Vol. 2, folio 47–49 (Lambeth Palace Archives).

4. *Ibid.*

5. *Ibid.*

6. *Ibid.* Rather surprisingly even the *Record*, 13 January 1848, supported Hampden's appointment.

7. Bodleian Library Library MS Wilberforce d 47, letter No. 8, Sumner to Wilberforce.

8. Ashwell A.R., *Life of the Rt Revd Samuel Wilberforce* (John Murray, 1880), Vol. 1, p. 435.

9. Letter from Prince Albert to Lord John Russell, 14 February 1848, Royal Archives, Windsor Castle, C. 18.
10. Wilberforce R.G., *Life of the Rt Revd Samuel Wilberforce*, (John Murray, 1881), Vol. 2, p. 6.
11. The *Record*, 13 March 1848.
12. For a detailed report see *The Illustrated London News*, 6 May 1848. See also *Times* (London), 29 April 1848. See also *Kentish Gazette*, 2 May 1848.
13. The *Record*, 3 May 1848. See also *Times* (London), 29 April 1848. See also The *Kentish Gazette*, 2 May 1848.
14. Newsome D., *The Parting of Friends* (John Murray, 1966), p. 301.
15. Sumner G.R., *Life of Charles Richard Sumner* (John Murray, 1876), p. 320.
16. *The Illustrated London News*, 6 May 1848.
17. *The Record*, 17 February 1848.
18. Sumner J.B., *Act Book*, Volume 1, p. 20 (Lambeth Palace Archives).
19. Sumner to Russell, August 1850, Russell Papers 8F 276–277.
20. *British Magazine*, February 1849.
21. See Sumner J.B., *Correspondence with William Maskell* (Lambeth Palace Archives) MS 37,824, folio 89. Sumner to Maskell, 26 April 1851.
22. *Ibid.*, MS 37,824, folios 208–12.
23. *Ibid.*
24. *Ibid.* folio 216.
25. *Christian Observer*, October 1851.
26. Sumner J.B. to Lord John Russell, 13 February 1851, PRO MS 9B79.
27. *Christian Observer*, November 1856.
28. Sumner J.B., *The Charge of John Bird Lord Archbishop of Canterbury to the Clergy of the Diocese at his Visitation 1853* (London, J. Hatchard & Son, 1853), p. 33.
29. *Ibid.*, p. 41.
30. *Ibid.*, p. 32.
31. *Christian Observer*, April 1859.
32. *Ibid.*, April 1859.
33. Queen Victoria to Sumner, Russell Papers PRO MS D9K pp. 54–57.
34. See Scotland, N.A.D., entry for George Cornelius Gorham in *Dictionary of the Earlier Evangelical Party* (Blackwell, 1995).

35. Chadwick O., *The Victorian Church* (A. & C. Black, 1966), Part 1, p. 261.
36. *Christian Observer*, November 1850.
37. Chadwick O., *op. cit.*, Part 1, p. 41.
38. *Christian Observer*, August 1851.
39. Lord John Russell, *Letter Book 1847–51*, MS ENG LETTERS.
40. Sumner J.B., *Charge to the Clergy of the Diocese at his Visitation 1853*, (J. Hatchard & Son, 1853), p. 11.
41. Sumner J.B. to Lord Aberdeen, 3 July 1854, *Aberdeen Papers* (British Museum) Vol. CLVII 43, 195 folio 119.
42. *Ibid.*
43. See Wilberforce R.G., *Life of the Right Reverend Samuel Wilber-force* (John Murray, 1880–1882), Vol. 2, p.138; Sumner J.B. to Lord Aberdeen, *Aberdeen Papers* (British Museum) Vol. CLVII, Add. MS 43, 195 folio 154.
44. *Ibid.*, folio 158.
45. For two exceptions see *Chronicle of Convocation*, 14 February 1859 Sumner spoke on pew rents; 8 June 1860 Sumner spoke on missionary bishops.
46. See Scotland, N.A.D., 'Essays and Reviews and the Reaction of Anglican Churchmen', *Downside Review*, April 1990, pp. 146–156.
47. Wilson, H.B., *Essays and Reviews* (J.W. Parker & Son, Oxford, 1860), p. 175.
48. *Ibid.*, p. 377.
49. See Scotland N.A.D., *op. cit.*, p. 148.
50. See Reardon B.M.G., *From Coleridge to Gore* (Longman, London, 1971), p. 340.
51. *Christian Observer*, June 1860.
52. Davidson R.T. and Benham W., *Campbell Tait* (London, Macmillan, 1891), Vol. I, pp. 281–282.
53. Sumner J.B. letter to a Dorsetshire Rural Deanery (Lambeth) 12 February 1861, *ibid.*, p. 282.
54. Crowther M.A., *The Church Embattled*, (Exeter, David and Charles, 1970), p. 158.
55. Lord John Russell to Sumner 14 November 1848, Bodleian Library, MS D307, pp. 133–4.
56. Sumner to Lord John Russell, 14 January 1850, PRO MS 8C260–261.

57. Scotland N.A.D., 'John Bird Sumner in Parliament', *Anvil*, Vol. 7, 2 November 1990, p. 261.

58. Lord John Russell to Sumner, 4 April 1859, PRO MS 9K, 54–57.

59. Sumner to T.S. Estcourt 17 July 1861, *Estcourt Papers*, Gloucester County Archives MSD 1571X86.

60. See Jenkins R.C., *Diocesan Histories: Canterbury* (London, SPCK, 1880), p. 407 f.

61. See also Sumner J.B., *The Charge of John Bird, Lord Archbishop of Canterbury to the Clergy of the Diocese at His Primary Visitation of 1853* (London, J. Hatchard, 1849), p. 5.

62. *Ibid.*, pp. 30–31.

63. *Ibid.*, p. 8. See also *Canterbury National Schools Minute Book* (Diocesan Archives MS U/9/F/1).

64. Sumner J.B., *op. cit.*, p. 8.

65. See for example *Acts of Consecration Book 1848–55* (Diocesan Archives, Canterbury), 18 September 1851 and *Consecration Acts Book* 1860–69 (Diocesan Archives, Canterbury), 20 August 1862.

66. Sumner J.B., *The Charge of John Bird, Lord Archbishop of Canterbury to the Clergy of the Diocese at His Visitation 1853* (London, J. Hatchard, 1853), p. 5.

67. This figure is computed from the deeds of consecration. In one or two cases where the number of sittings is not given, an average figure has been inserted.

68. Sumner J.B., *The Charge of John Bird, Lord Archbishop of Canterbury to the Clergy of the Diocese at His Visitation, 1857* (London, Thomas Hatchard, 1857), p. 11.

69. *Ibid.*, p. 14.

70. *Ibid.*, pp. 12–13.

71. Sumner J.B., *The Charge of John Bird, Lord Archbishop of Canterbury to the Clergy of the Diocese at His Primary Visitation, 1849* (London, Thomas Hatchard, 1849), p. 15.

72. *Ibid.*, p. 16.

73. Boggis R.J.E., *A History of St Augustine's College Canterbury* (Cross & Jackman), 1907), p. 90.

74. Sumner J.B., *The Charge of John Bird Lord Archbishop of Canterbury to the Clergy of the Diocese at His Visitation 1857* (London, Thomas Hatchard, 1857), p. 2.

75. *The Kentish Gazette*, 2 May 1848. See the account of his Sermon in Canterbury Cathedral on the Sunday following his enthronement.

76. Jenkins R.C., *Diocesan Histories: Canterbury* (London, SPCK, 1880), p. 407.

77. *Ibid.*, p. 408.

9

Archbishop
of the Colonial Church

The middle years of the nineteenth century 1840–70 are generally seen as a 'colonial' rather than 'imperialist' era in so far as British government policy was concerned. This was also a period in which emigration to the new lands of the empire was to increase considerably, reaching a high point in the last quarter of the nineteenth century.[1] This growth in emigration was parallelled by a growth in the Anglican communion, which by the end of the nineteenth century was reckoned to number in excess of 16,000,000.[2] It had therefore become apparent that what was needed was the establishment of a self-governing self-propagating, and self-supporting colonial Church. Sumner came to the helm of the Anglican Communion at a crucial moment. Much would be demanded of him in terms of energy, negotiation and planning.

Sumner's policies with regard to mission and the Colonial Church are illuminated by the extant records of his detailed correspondence with the third Earl Grey as Colonial Office Secretary, as well as by a variety of missionary society papers, letters and Annual Reports. On 3 July 1851 Sumner wrote to Earl Grey that 'the Colonial Churches... are becoming of increased importance through the large additions annually made to the population'. For that reason he went on to proffer his full support for the proposed commissions of inquiry into the work of the Church in various colonies.[3]

General Policy

Sumner's general policy with regard to mission and the Colonial Church can be characterised as expansionism. The 'vision' to extend and to build which he had developed in his Chester Diocese he now carried with him in his strategy for the Colonial Churches. He committed himself to a policy of subdividing existing dioceses to create newer more manageable structures. He also worked for the establishment of Metropolitan sees in Australia, New Zealand and Canada. Among other sees which Sumner had a direct hand in establishing were Freetown in 1849, Victoria (Hong Kong) in 1849, Rupert's Land in 1849, Natal in 1850, Nova Scotia in 1851, and Wellington and Nelson in 1858. On 10 May 1850 Sumner wrote to Earl Grey of the need for new sees in New Zealand and Canada. The Earl replied that he was happy to comply with those proposals as soon as the endowments had been provided.[4] Again in December 1850 Sumner wrote to Earl Grey of the desperate need to subdivide the Diocese of Cape Town by creating a new see of Natal. 'The fact', he wrote, 'that Bishop Grey has been employed for 9 months in a visitation is a sufficient proof of the necessity of the case'.[5] Earl Grey replied the following week agreeing to Sumner's proposal to upgrade the status of the Archdeaconry of Natal to that of a bishopric.[6]

In general terms Grey and the Colonial office seemed happy to subscribe to Sumner's strategy of expansion. They were however quick to draw his attention to the costs involved and to impress upon him that no scheme for new sees or other developments in the Colonial dioceses could be contemplated unless the requisite funds had first been raised.[7] An example of this approach was Earl Grey's response to Sumner's request for a division of the diocese of Montreal: 'I have to remind your Grace that before any further step can be taken it is necessary that it should be shown to me that a permanent and secure endowment has been provided for a second bishop.'[8]

By the time of Sumner's elevation to the primacy, the Church of England was solidifying into more readily definable party groupings each with their own distinctive theology and ceremonial. Relevant to the question of mission were two basic emerging opinions regarding the nature of the Church. High Churchmen who regarded bishops as of the *plene esse* of the Church came increasingly to the view that the bishop was central to mission. As they saw it, Anglican missions should be spearheaded by specially chosen missionary bishops. Alongside this, where colonies had already been established and ex-patriates were now settled with their own places of worship, it became the first priority to incorporate them within a diocesan structure. High Churchmen therefore constantly urged on the government the need to establish new Colonial dioceses. Their missionary societies devoted much time and energy to raising endowments for new bishoprics.

Among those who represented this higher view of episcopacy were men such as Joshua Watson, the leader of the 'Hackney Phalanx', Edward Pusey, and Bishop Samuel Wilberforce who came to have an increasing empathy with high-Church principles. In his *History of the Protestant Episcopal Church in America*, Wilberforce wrote: 'Evangelical truth with apostolic order—the Gospel in the Church. There must be no paring down... that form of Church order which Christ has appointed'.[9] In 1853 Samuel Wilberforce passed through the House of Lords a *Colonial Church Bill* and a *Missionary Bishops Bill* both of which were designed to raise the level, status and commitment to episcopacy in the Churches of the Empire. However both bills were defeated in the Commons, one being withdrawn and the other thrown out. This was mainly through the efforts of Arthur Kinnaird who acted on behalf of the evangelical leaders whose fear of growing ritualistic tendencies drove them to extremes of erastianism.[10] Wilberforce frequently made the point that the colonial Churches should not be denied the system of episcopal superintendence which was so highly valued at home. For example in his sermon in Westminster Abbey on the occasion of the third Jubilee of the SPG he declared:

> There must be no choosing by us in which part of Christ's
> appointments we will select for use: no deeming that Bishops
> may be needful at home, but that presbyters will suffice for
> foreign work. There must be a perception that for this great

attempt, the very best of all instruments of service are required.[11]

Speaking in a Convocation debate in June 1860 he put the motion for this very reason 'that the Ven. Archdeacon Mackenzie who had been selected to lead a mission to Southern Central Africa be admitted into the episcopal order before he be sent forth to the heathen'.[12] Significantly, later in the same debate, Sumner, who rarely spoke in Convocation, tempered Wilberforce's position. He agreed that it might well be desirable to have a mission led by a bishop 'but it does not by any means say that missions which are not so headed may not be advisable in many cases'.[13]

In these words Sumner represented the views of many low churchman and evangelicals. Like the high churchmen they valued bishops and saw the importance of establishing indigenous diocesan structures. However, they were less urgent in their pleas for an immediate episcopal presence in every locality in which Church missionaries were operative. Some evangelicals such as Henry Venn, felt that the first stages of mission were better left to the unhindered pioneer missionary or the planning of the missionary Society.

Associated with these two differing opinions of episcopacy and its role in mission were two views about the manner in which the Colonial dioceses should operate. High churchmen who already resented the increasing government interference with Church of England rights and privileges, put the case that Colonial dioceses should be self-governing. Samuel Wilberforce's *Colonial Churches Bill* had proposed to authorise bishops, clergy and laity in the Colonies to meet together and make whatever ecclesiastical relations they might deem necessary, provided that the standards of faith and worship and the supremacy of the crown were duly maintained'.[14] Evangelicals such as Henry Venn, the General Secretary of CMS, Edward Bickersteth and John Bird Sumner urged that the Colonial Churches should have less autonomy and that their dioceses should be more directly under the influence of the British Government and the Colonial Office. In this way they felt that there was also less likelihood of the excesses of the Oxford Movement being replicated on foreign soil. Furthermore by this procedure they believed that the working of individual missionaries and their societies would be better safeguarded. CMS, for example, found that they could not place their missionaries under the authority of Bishop Robert Gray in Cape Town on account of his rigidly high-Church principles.[15]

Sumner's Views on Missionary Societies

Those churchmen whose views on mission and the Colonial Church accorded with a higher view of episcopacy frequently urged the necessity of amalgamating all the Church of England foreign missionary societies and bringing them under one umbrella. As far as most of them were concerned such a governing authority would be Convocation. By this means they hoped to present a more unified version of Anglicanism on the foreign fields which would be evangelical in proclamation and Catholic in Church order.

As early as the 1840s Samuel Wilberforce, when Archdeacon of Surrey, had suggested a combination of SPG, SPCK, the Clergy Aid Society (later the Additional Curates Society), the Church Building Society, the National Society, the CMS and CPAS. At this earlier point in time the motivation stemmed from the fact that there had emerged a number of more vigorous bishops who had shown much greater devotion to duty and who had demonstrated more ability and efficiency in their administration. In addition, the renewal of rural deaneries had created what was felt to be a convenient local tier of organisation through which missionary monies could be raised and distributed.

However, as the century progressed incidences of ritualism and ritual prosecution increased, causing the gap between 'high' and 'low' church to widen. This began to alienate many low churchmen from the SPG who in consequence started to fear a significant decline in their financial support. It was this which prompted the society in its Annual Report of 1850 'once again, and most earnestly, [to] call attention to the great and pressing need of uniting together all members of the Church in furtherance of the holy work of Missions'.[16] Another blow ensued for the SPG in 1857 with the withdrawal of the Queen's Letter. Up until this time SPG which had been founded by Royal Charter, enjoyed the privilege of a triennial letter from the monarch urging the people of England to subscribe to its work. The reasons behind the Queen's unexpected refusal to issue any further letters were made clear. Her action inevitably increased the clamour for an amalgamation of missionary societies and an equitable distribution of funds raised in the individual parishes.

Sumner had always stood for the independence and authority of individual missionary societies. As early as his speech at the 1840 Annual General Meeting of the CMS he strenuously opposed the proposal to bring all missionary societies together in one church-organised body.[17] He reiterated the same position in his 1852 *Charge to the Diocese of Canterbury*.

> Will anyone, who has the least acquaintance with the machinery of these great societies, propose that they should be interfered with, or... be... under a body like Convocation?'[18]

Sumner went on to say that if missionary work was suddenly placed under Convocation it would take away spontaneity. Many of the great early Church Missions were, as he pointed out, spontaneously prompted by the Holy Spirit. He concluded that 'Convocation if ever led to interfere with those societies, certainly could not contribute to their prosperity: and it would probably throw them into confusion'.[19] Despite these forthright words from the Primate, the issue did not die away. Three years later Henry Venn, the CMS general secretary, found himself explaining in a letter to Sir Henry Thornton the reasons why he did not wish his society to be included with three other missionary societies in an Archiepiscopal fund-raising letter. Venn wrote that:

> ... it has always been the unanimous opinion that a Queen's licence or an Archbishop's letter once in three or even once in two years would be disadvantageous to our cause—we have hard work to keep up annual sermons... yet all our success depends upon keeping the subject constantly before the people.[20]

Yet although Sumner held that it was important for individual missionary societies to maintain their distinctiveness and independence, he nevertheless grasped the importance of trying to keep a broad-based unity between the diverse elements of the growing world-wide Anglican communion. In particular, Sumner recognised that American independence had caused a rift between the American clergy and their English counterparts. In an attempt to bring about reconciliation, Sumner made use of the third jubilee of the SPG in March 1851. As the Society's President, he issued a written plea for reconciliation to all American bishops. He submitted to them:

> ... whether, in a time of controversy and division, the close communion which binds the Churches of America and England in one, would not be strikingly manifested to the world, if everyone of their dioceses were to take part in commemorating the foundation of the oldest Missionary Society of the Reformed Church, a society which, from its beginnings in New England, has extended its operations into all parts of the world, from the Ganges to Lake Huron and from New Zealand to Labrador.[21]

No gift was asked beyond 'Christian sympathy and prayer'. The American bishops responded exceedingly warmly to Sumner's invitation.[22] Their answers were so full of gratitude and warm feelings both to the society and to the Church at large that they occupied 23 pages of the Annual Report of 1851.

At the request which the Society had made 'with a view to fuller and more complete intercommunion between the distant portions of the Church', two American bishops were delegated to take part in the conclusion of the Jubilee year. The Bishop of Western New York preached at St James' Piccadilly on 15 June 1852 and the Bishop of Michigan in St Paul's Cathedral on the following day. The latter occasion was the first time an anniversary sermon was delivered by an American bishop.

By this gracious gesture Sumner to some extent at least, opened up the way for the development of the Lambeth Conferences. The first initial move in this direction came in the response of Bishop Hopkins of Vermont. He expressed the gratitude of American churchmen when 'a Prelate of our revered mother church speaks, as your grace has been pleased to do, of the 'close communion which binds the Churches of America and England'. He went on to say 'How natural and reasonable would it seem to be, if "in a time of controversy and division", there would be a council of all the bishops in communion with your Grace!'[23] Although Sumner did not take up Hopkins' suggestion of 'a council of all the bishops' in his communion, reconciliation overtures towards the American Church sowed the seeds which paved the way from the Lambeth Conferences.

Sumner's Relationship with CMS and SPG

Of all the missionary societies, Sumner's closest affinity was with the *Church Missionary Society*. It was born of the endeavours of the Simeonite School to which he had always belonged. In his early days as a Berkshire incumbent Sumner had been an active supporter of the Reading branch of the CMS. Now as archbishop he enjoyed the company of Henry Venn, the Society's general secretary. In fact Venn had been one of Sumner's closest friends for many years and in his CMS correspondence Venn makes frequent reference to his visits to Lambeth and his talks with Sumner. The following are typical anecdotes. To the Bishop of Madras he wrote: 'I dined at Lambeth on Friday and found the Archbishop as calm and as cheerful as ever.'[24] Again to the Bishop of Calcutta: 'I spent two days last week with the Archbishop at Addington.'[25] In fact, Venn viewed Sumner's elevation to the primacy as 'the tide running in our favour'.[26] He continued: 'At the same time the identity in feeling and in the aim of our beloved Archbishop and his cordial assistance in every respect is a mighty advantage to our cause. We must all unite in prayer that as a society we may not be found wanting.'[27]

The assistance which Sumner was able to give extended into several areas of the Society's work. These included bringing the Society and the episcopate into a closer working relationship and support for its policy of 'nativisation'.

In the early days of its existence CMS had experienced an extended period of uneasy tension with the episcopate. This was particularly with the overseas episcopate. There had been two brushes over the question of licensing ordained CMS missionaries. These concerned Bishop Daniel Wilson in India and Bishop James Broughton. CMS missionaries in the foreign field and their affairs were handled by Corresponding Committees which usually consisted of leading local laymen. These local CMS committees tended to deal directly with the Colonial governments bypassing the bishops in whose dioceses they operated. Bishops such as Wilson and Broughton stood out against such action and contended that such missionaries must be licensed by them and operate under their aegis.

CMS, and Henry Venn in particular, argued that CMS's position in the foreign field should be at least as equal to that of the 'Lay Patron' at home. 'The CMS', it was held, 'should be able to present men for a licence to any particular station and, as with 'Mr Simeon's trustees... if nothing appeared against the candidate's orthodoxy, morals and ability the nominee is automatically instituted'.[28]

Other struggles followed in which CMS stood out for the independence of catechists from episcopal control by licence, for the right of the society to determine the location of its missionaries, for the freedom of missionaries from direct episcopal superintendence over adult baptisms, and for the right of CMS to present candidates for ordination prepared solely at their own training institution.

All these issues caused considerable tension between CMS and the episcopate. Henry Venn (1796–1873) who held the office of General Secretary from 1841 to 72, began to develop a more eirenical and conciliatory policy. Much of this change was due to a number of English bishops taking office as CMS Vice-presidents in the early 1840s. The steady patronage which Sumner and his brother Charles gave to CMS as Vice-presidents, Anniversary preachers and AGM Speakers, did a great to heal this breach. John Bird also on occasion, ordained CMS candidates for the foreign fields.

As General Secretary of CMS , Henry Venn formulated a policy of establishing 'self-governing, self-sustaining and self-propagating' indigenous local churches. This led him to promote a policy of 'nativisation', a strategy which Sumner was happy to endorse. In 1852 for example, Venn sought to establish an arrangement whereby the new Diocese of Sierra Leone should support its own native pastors. He drew up 'Articles of Arrangement' between the Society and the archbishopric to which Sumner, along with Bishop Blomfield, readily assented.[29] Sumner however had the foresight to see the need to avoid foisting the finer details of the Church of England's ecclesiastical machinery on the outbacks of West Africa. He wrote to Venn that he saw 'no sort of necessity anywhere, in a new diocese' for Cathedral, Dean and Canons. Indeed he continued, 'nowhere less than in Sierra Leone... The Natives would find themselves much at a loss in the managements of a Chapter'.[30]

The other major nineteenth-century missionary Society supported by the Church of England was the SPG which had been founded by Royal Charter in 1701. In earlier times the Society had been supported by low-churchmen as well as those of high-church views. However, with the emergence of ritualism in the 1840s and 50s, the gulf between high and low-church parties started to widen once again. Many low churchmen began to feel more comfortable with the vigorous endeavours of the Church Missionary Society. But at this time when others were leaving the SPG, Sumner remained an active supporter of the Society and of its literary arm, the SPCK. In his days at Chester Sumner had subscribed to the *Chester District Association for the Society of the Propagation of the Gospel*[31] and in 1835 preached a sermon at Trinity Church Chester on the Society's behalf. Despite his very busy schedule Sumner took the chair at almost every one of the twice-yearly meetings of the Chester diocesan SPCK.[32]

John Bird preached the SPG Anniversary Sermon in 1834 and later presided over its 150th anniversary celebrations in June 1851. Sumner's continuing support for both the SPG and SPCK typify his gracious open-minded spirit. When Sumner died in 1862 the next Annual General meeting of the SPG placed on record:

... the large debt of gratitude which it owes to its president, Archbishop Sumner, for the kindly interest with which he uniformly enriched its welfare, his liberal contribution to its funds, his ever-ready co-operation in the great designs of the Society, his frequent public testimony to the vast importance of its Missionary operations, and its consequent claims for support upon all the members of the Church.[33]

The SPCK at its 1862 AGM also placed on record 'its sense of the great loss', which not only the Society itself, but the Church at large has sustained'. The Standing Committee went on to speak of 'the deep interest which the late Archbishop always evinced in the welfare of this Society.[34]

John Bird Sumner did all within his power to encourage both of the Church of England's two main foreign missionary Societies, and by his broad-minded support he kept open the lines of communication between them. Although it is true to say that his spirit was closer to those who were identified with the CMS, in the main Sumner avoided using his high office to promote the interests of his own party. His vision was a broad one, and he saw beyond the localised internal politics of the Church of England to the needs of the much greater and more rapidly growing overseas Anglican Communion. As he put it in a letter to Bishop Samuel Wilberforce who criticised him on more than one occasion: 'my thoughts were not turned to this Society or the other, but the cause in which the Society is engaged.[35]

Sumner and the Appointment of Colonial Bishops

One matter which was closely related with Sumner's dealings with the CMS and SPG, was the appointment of overseas bishops. In an age which was starting to become aware of the scandal of a divided Church on the mission field, Sumner displayed wisdom and tact. On some occasions he consulted the SPG Committee, but at other times he sought advice from Henry Venn. Sometimes he consulted both over the same appointment. This was particularly so in the case of the Indian episcopate.[36] One of the first of such foreign appointments was that of the Revd George Smith, a pioneer missionary to China, who was appointed to the new bishopric of Victoria (Hong Kong).[37] The establishment of this see had been strongly urged

on the Government by Lord Chichester and Henry Venn, and
an endowment was provided largely through the generosity of
an anonymous supporter of the SPG and SPCK. This fact
notwithstanding, Venn's influence with Sumner and the Colonial office secured the position for Smith. Sumner's correspondence with Earl Grey at the Colonial office is illustrative of the
great deal of trouble which he took over Colonial Church
matters. He wrote from Addington on 20 December that 'the
person who appears, after much inquiry, to be the best suited
for so difficult a post is the Revd George Smith who I understand has already been made known to you'. Sumner continued:
'his zeal, piety and talent are unquestionable and I believe that
he has proved himself to be possessed of much skill in manag-
ing matters of business in official situations, which in such a
new position must be a very important qualification'.[38] Earl
Grey replied at the beginning of the following month that Smith
was not a suitable candidate 'having inveighed in the pulpit
against the Colonial Government'. The issue concerned Colonial police regulations which he apparently regarded as 'unduly
severe' towards the Chinese.[39] Sumner evidently took time to
consult Henry Venn on the matter and replied the next week as
follows:

> I hope that I am not trespassing against any new rule, in sending
> the enclosed papers, which I have received from Mr Venn,
> Secretary of the Church Missionary Society, in vindication of
> that part of Mr Smith's conduct to which objection has been
> taken. The documents appear alarming in bulk, but will be soon
> glanced over.[40]

Earl Grey replied by return that he was entirely happy with
Sumner's explanation. This prompted a further communication
from Sumner on Smith's behalf that 'if there are no serious
objections against him, he certainly has qualifications for the
appointment which no one else possesses'. Sumner continued
that he had received the following sentences from a very
judicious friend: 'Smith seems marked out for China, and the
opportunities I have had of seeing him satisfy me that he is a
superior man'.[41] Smith was duly consecrated on 29 May 1849.[42]
Yates commented on Smith's consecration that it was 'one of a

number of appointments sympathetic to CMS made during J.B. Sumner's period of office as Archbishop of Canterbury'.[43] A cursory glance at some of those raised to episcopal office in the Colonial Church by Sumner indicates the rightness of Yates' assessment of the matter.

In 1851 Sumner entered into a fairly detailed correspondence over the appointment of the new bishop for the see of Nova Scotia. His exchange of letters with Earl Grey is of interest because it shows that Sumner was clearly sensitive to the issues of Churchmanship and Church parties. In November 1850 he received a letter from the Earl informing him that a Herbert Binney had made a private application for the position of Bishopric of Nova Scotia. He asks Sumner for his opinion of him.[44] Sumner replied two days later that he had 'received a most unqualified recommendation in his favour from Dr Cotton, Provost of his College whose opinion is greatly to be depended on'. Sumner concluded by asking Earl Grey to let him know if he 'should incline in Mr Binney's favour'.[45] Sumner appears not to have received any further correspondence on the matter from the Earl. On 12 December however, he received a letter from the Dean of his own Cathedral Church commending the Revd Cecil Wynter 'a connexion of his' for the post. He wrote immediately to Earl Grey concerning Wynter stating that 'his appointment will be generally satisfactory'.[46] Earl Grey replied a fortnight later that the nomination of Binney 'would be the most satisfactory to the Colony from his family connection with it'.[47] Sumner replied almost immediately that his subsequent recommendation of Wynter was known to the Society of the Propagation of the Gospel which furnishes whatever funds there are for the maintenance of the Bishop'. 'Another person', he maintained, 'is likely to be unfavourably received by the subscribers of the Society'.[48] The Earl responded pointing out that Sumner's letter of 9 November, had contained 'so unqualified an expression of the fitness of Mr Binney for the appointment' that he had considered it 'my duty to submit his name to H. Majesty by whom the appointment has been approved'.[49] As things turned Herbert Binney (*d.* 1887) proved an able Bishop of Nova Scotia who 'gave statesmanlike leadership and guidance to his Diocese for twenty-six years'.[50] On account of his high-Church views he came to be regarded as an SPG bishop.[51]

Generally speaking the bishops who were appointed to Colonial sees during Sumner's primacy proved to be wise men who made effective contributions in their respective sees. George Smith (*d.* 1878), first bishop of Victoria, although not successful in some of his projects, was an untiring traveller whose influence was highly valued.[52] In March 1849 Sumner solicited the appointment of the Revd David Anderson as Bishop of Rupert's Land in Canada. He informed Earl Grey that Anderson 'was for many years in my Diocese of Chester and is a person whom I can very confidently recommend.'[53] Anderson, 'a highly esteemed evangelical clergyman',[54] was consecrated in Canterbury Cathedral and proved to be a great traveller and encourager under whose leadership new mission stations were opened up and the Bible translated into Native American languages.[55]

Another Canadian bishop who received office on Sumner's recommendation was Francis Fulford (1803–68) who was consecrated first bishop of the new Diocese of Montreal in Westminster Abbey in July 1850. Fulford proved a very able bishop and such were his wide abilities in leadership and administration that in 1860 the Queen issued letters patent promoting him to the office of Metropolitan of Canada.[56]

In 1856 Sumner caused a certain amount of alarm in his appointment of an evangelical, the Revd Henry Cotterill, to succeed John Armstrong as Bishop of Grahamstown.[57] Bishop Gray of Capetown, the Metropolitan see, was not consulted and was furious at the appointment. It was felt that Sumner had either acted on the advice of Lord Shaftesbury, the evangelical philanthropist, or had been persuaded to it by communications from a dissident congregation in Port Elizabeth.[58] As things turned out however, Bishop Gray found in Cotterill 'a wise and sympathetic colleague' who moved his diocese away from Erastian policies towards self-government by forming his own Synod in 1858.[59] Another evangelical, Frederick Barker (1808–1882), owed his appointment as Bishop of Sydney to Sumner.

Barker had served in Sumner's diocese at Upton by Birkenhead and as incumbent of St Mary, Edgehill, in Liverpool. Barker was consecrated by Sumner at Lambeth Parish Church on St Andrew's Day 1854. Barker initiated an extensive Church building programme which included the erection of a 'Cathedral and was based on Sumner's Chester strategy. Like Sumner, Barker also concerned himself with scriptural education and the building of schools. He returned to England on three occasions to raise funds for his diocese and proved himself a very effective Church leader.[60]

One of Sumner's last appointments to a colonial see was that of Frederick Gell to Madras in 1861.[61] Like the other bishops mentioned above, Gell also proved himself to be a very effective administrator. His diocese had a larger number of clergy than any other overseas Anglican diocese.[62] Bishop Gell continued at Madras for 37 years, his episcopacy far exceeding in length that of any other Indian bishop.[63]

In evaluating Sumner's appointment to the colonial episcopate, several factors emerge. First a number of these appointments appear to have been sympathetic to the designs of CMS.[64] But having made this point, it is clear that Sumner also showed himself to be sympathetic to the endeavours of the SPG and anti-Erastian high Churchmen such as his relative Samuel Wilberforce, the Bishop of Oxford. The vast majority of those whom Sumner appointed of either party proved themselves to be able and effective Church leaders, although there were doubtless exceptions.[65]

Conclusion

Sumner took the reins of the Colonial Church at what was clearly a crucial period in its development. His fourteen-year term of office occurred at a time when the Empire was developing rapidly, and he saw clearly the vital necessity of ensuring that the Church's organisation and administration grew at a sufficient pace to provide for the needs of the increasing population. This led him to foster a strategy of creating new dioceses and establishing Metropolitan sees. Although his sympathies

were not those of an anti-erastian high Churchmen, he nevertheless allowed Colonial bishops to establish their own Synods
and to govern their own affairs wherever possible. Perhaps in
the end history will judge that Sumner's greatest service to the
Colonial Church was his overture of reconciliation to the American bishops at the SPG's 150th Anniversary. This event seems
to have anticipated the emergence of the Lambeth Conferences
and the birth and conscious growth in identity of the world-wide
Anglican Communion.

Notes

1. See for example Horn P.L.R., 'Agricultural Trade Unionism and
   Emigration 1872–1881' *The Historical Journal* XV, (1972) pp.
   87–102.
2. In 1837 the number of British people living in the colonies was a
   mere 4,000,000. By 1900 it was more than 16,000,000. See Elliot
   Binns, L.E., *Religion in the Victorian Era* (London, Lutterworth
   Press, 1964) p. 394.
3. See *The Earl Grey Papers* (3rd Earl), Dept of Palaeography, University of Durham.
4. 3rd Earl Grey to Sumner J.B., 13 May 1850.
5. Sumner J.B. to 3rd Earl Grey, 27 December 1850.
6. 3rd Earl Grey to Sumner J.B., 2 January 1851.
7. See for example 3rd Earl Grey to Sumner, 2 January 1850 and 19
   January, 1850.
8. 3rd Earl Grey to Sumner J.B., 2 January 1850.
9. Cited Newsome D., *The Parting of Friends* (John Murray, 1966) p.
   216.
10. Stock E., *History of the Church Missionary Society* (CMS, 1899)
    Vol. 2, p. 13.
11. *Annual Report of SPG*, 1852, p. xxxiv.
12. *Chronicle of Convocation* (London, 1860) 8 June, 1860, p. 295.
13. *Ibid.*, p. 301.
14. Stock E., *op. cit.*, Vol. 2, p.13.
15. Thompson H.P., *Into All Lands* (London, SPCK, 1851), p. 116.
16. *Annual Report of SPG* (1850), p. cxvii.
17. See *Annual Report of CMS*, 1840.

18. Sumner J.B., *The Charge of John Bird Lord Archbishop of Canterbury to the Clergy of the Diocese at His Visitation* (London, J. Hatchard & Son, 1853), p. 20.

19. *Ibid.*, p. 23.

20. Venn H. to Sir Henry Thornton, Bart, 31 July 1856 MS G/AC1/39, CMS Archives, University of Birmingham.

21. Pascoe C.F., *Two Hundred Years of the SPG 1701–1900* (London, SPG, 1901), Vol. 1, p. 1.

22. *Ibid.*, p. 81.

23. See Stephenson, A.M.G., *Anglicanism and the Lambeth Conferences* (London, SPCK, 1978) pp. 19–21.

24. Venn H. to Bishop of Madras, 19 March 1850, *South India Letter Book* Vol. 5, pp. 3–4.

25. Venn H. to Bishop of Calcutta 24 August 1849, *North India Letter Book* Vol. 3, p. 452.

26. Venn H. to Revd G.G. Cuthbert, 19th August 1848, *ibid.*, pp. 422–424, p.169.

27. *Ibid.*, p. 422–424.

28. Yates T.E., *Venn and Victorian Bishops* (Uppsala, Swedish Institute of Missionary Studies, 1978), p. 35.

29. Stock E., *op. cit.*, Vol. 2, p. 416.

30. Yates T., *op. cit.*, p. 116.

31. See for example *Chester District Association for the Society of the Propagation of the Gospel Minute Book 1831–1881*, for 1831 (Chester Diocesan Record Office MS EDD 1/19).

32. See *Minute Book of Chester Diocesan SPCK,* (Chester Diocesan Record Office) MS EDD 1/18.

33. *SPG Annual General Report*, 1863, p. 25.

34. *SPCK Minute Book 1860–6*, Tuesday 7 October 1862. See also note 33 of chapter 10.

35. Sumner J.B. to Samuel Wilberforce, 8 September 1856 (Bodleian Library MS Wilberforce d. 47 item 50).

36. See Stock E., *op. cit.*, Vol. 2, p. 647.

37. *Ibid.*, Vol. 1, p. 473.

38. Sumner J.B. to 3rd Earl Grey, 20 December 1848.

39. 3rd Earl Grey to Sumner J.B., 2 January 1849.

40. Sumner J.B. to 3rd Earl Grey, 10 January 1849.

41. Sumner J.B. to 3rd Earl Grey 13 January 1849.

42. For Smith's consecration see Stock E., *op. cit.*, Vol. 1, p. 473.
43. Yates, T.E., *op. cit.*, p. 177.
44. 3rd Earl Grey to Sumner J.B., 7 November 1850.
45. Sumner J.B. to 3rd Earl Grey, 9 November 1850.
46. Sumner J.B. to 3rd Earl Grey, 7 February, 1851.
47. 3rd Earl Grey to Sumner J.B., 21 February 1851.
48. Sumner J.B. to Earl Grey, 24 February 1851.
49. 3rd Earl Grey to Sumner J.B., 25 February 1851.
50. For Binney's episcopate see Carrington P., *The Anglican Church in Canada* (Toronto, Collins, 1963) p. 184.
51. *Ibid.*, pp. 117–118.
52. See Stock E., *op. cit.*, Vol. 2, p. 309.
53. Sumner J.B. to 3rd Earl Grey, 14 March 1849.
54. Stock E, *op.cit.*, Vol. 2, p. 312.
55. *Ibid.*, Vol. 2, pp. 333–325. For Anderson see also *Dictionary of National Biography*.
56. Sumner J.B. to 3rd Earl Grey, 10 May 1850.
57. Thompson H.P., *op. cit.*, p. 296.
58. Hinchliff P., *The Anglican Church in South Africa: an account of the history and development of the Church of the Province of South Africa*, (Darton, Longman & Todd, 1963), pp. 58–61.
59. *Ibid.*, pp. 58–61.
60. For Frederick Barker see *Dictionary of National Biography*.
61. Stock E, *op. cit.*, Vol. 2, p. 647.
62. *Ibid.*, Vol. 2, p. 764.
63. *Ibid.*, Vol. 2, p. 275.
64. Yates T., *op. cit.*, p. 177.
65. For example J.W. Colenso, Bishop of Natal. See Stock, E., *op. cit.*, Vol. 2, p. 16.

10

John Bird Sumner

Reading through the obituary notices and the funeral sermons which were preached shortly after Sumner's death, one gains the impression that Sumner was at the time rated fairly high in the scale of Archbishops of Canterbury.[1] The *Times*, for example, did not class Sumner among the famous, but stated 'he may surely be ranked very high for his wisdom, for his kindliness, and for his devotion'.[2] Nevertheless it would be wrong to suggest that Sumner was without his critics both within his lifetime and subsequently.

Sumner's Critics

One of the accusations which was made most often against Sumner was that he was too much a party man. In the main this opinion emanated from high Churchmen who had little truck with anything which savoured of Erastianism, and tractarians who were on the receiving end of his outspoken attacks against their ritualistic innovations. J. Cave Brown for example spoke of Sumner's vehement opposition to the ritualists as robbing him of much respect.[3] Baring Gould's partisan writing treated Sumner as submissive and incompetent.'[4] At a slightly later point in time Archbishop Randall Davidson wondered whether perhaps something other than Sumner's 'earnest evangelical fervour' would have been more effective 'when the protagonists around him were men of the calibre of Robert Gray and Samuel Wilberforce, of Henry Phillpotts and Hugh McNeil, or even Charles Kingsley and Dean Hook'.[5] In fact, it was Samuel

Wilberforce, Sumner's own relative, who proved to be among
his more serious critics. He felt him to be indecisive and not
capable of fulfilling the onerous duties of his office. He wrote
to Gladstone in December 1851 'of the fearful weakness caused
by the character of the Primate'. It has of course to be recognised
that Wilberforce had seen himself as a serious contender for the
archbishopric, only to see Sumner gain preferment in his place.
He may therefore at this stage still have been nurturing the pain
of several disappointments.

One of the issues over which Wilberforce may have adjudged
Sumner to be weak was in his refusal to countenance the attempt
to allow convocation to be reactivated and once more permitted
to debate ecclesiastical business. Since 1717 the Crown had
refused Convocation this right. Sumner resisted the revival of
Convocations because in his view it called in question the
authority of the crown. He also felt that it would open up
divisive debates on faith and worship which would weaken the
Church. In the event his fears were proved groundless and much
of the subsequent debate in Convocation proved calm and
statesmanlike, and had a positive outcome in the Church's life.

It has also been maintained that the Gawthorne Affair demonstrated that Sumner was not very astute. It will be recalled
that in this instance the archbishop was duped into stating a
position on the nature of episcopacy which, when it was made
public, caused considerable offence. Other writers had urged
that Sumner was too mild in disposition and lacked the ability
to be decisive in moments of crisis such as occurred in the
Gorham controversy or at the publication of *Essays and Reviews*. Yet issues such as these are still difficult to assess, even
with the benefit of more than 100 years of subsequent history
on which to base one's reflections.

Another area in which Sumner was open to criticism was in
his economic and social theorising. In his early years he had
taught and influenced a whole generation that poverty was the
natural God-ordained lot of many in a well ordered society.
Indeed, he had gone further and spoken of poverty as 'an
honourable estate'. Sumner's early view that the sovereign God
ruled over the nation had led him to Christianise *laissez-faire*

economic and social theory. This resulted in a free market in which only the fittest could survive. At the beginning of the 1830s as a Poor Law Commissioner, Sumner changed his mind when he found that many poor would rather take parish relief than go in search of work. This led him to advocate, along with his fellow commissioners, the harsh work-house scheme of the 1834 Poor Law Act. To many poor people, the work house which separated husband and wife was one of the most inhuman institutions of the century. That a Christian like Sumner should have had a hand in its creation seemed totally reprehensible. Clearly John Bird Sumner had his weak points both as Bishop of Chester and later as primate, but they need to be counterbalanced in any appreciation of his achievements by his many positive assets.

Sumner's Vision to Reach People with the Christian Message

From his earliest days as a part-time curate in Windsor[6] up until his last years as archbishop, Sumner gave himself to the business of communicating the heart of the Christian message. As he put it in his charge of 1849, the greatest duty is to expound to people 'the truth as it is in Jesus and tell them words by which they and their house may be saved'.[7] As he contemplated the enormity of this task, Sumner showed himself able to think critically of the Church of England structures and to suggest positive and imaginative ways of reaching the unchurched. As country incumbent in Berkshire, Sumner had been more than content with the parochial system but as bishop of a sprawling industrial diocese with burgeoning towns and rapidly increasing population, he soon became one of its most effective critics. Referring to the parish system in his charge to the Clergy of Chester he declared: 'Our ecclesiastical divisions are imperfect and inconvenient.[8] He went on to say: 'If we wait till all difficulties are smoothed, we shall wait till the world passes away.'[9] In the main, he sought to overcome the rigidity of parochial boundaries by promoting the building of Chapels of ease within existing urban parishes.[10]

The longer he contemplated the difficulties of communicating the Christian faith in a secularising urban culture, the more
he became convinced that ecclesiastical buildings were not a
suitable or endearing venue for ordinary working people. 'It's
too big a jump for such people', he claimed. 'The only hope is
that we carry our message to them.' He went on to recommend
the use of cottages and schoolrooms.[11] In 1858 Sumner introduced the third reading of *Church of England Special Services
Bill* which aimed to 'provide more suitable forms of worship
for the populous working class districts'.[12] For this reason, he
later spoke strongly in favour of Lord Shaftesbury's bill which
proposed that Church of England clergy be allowed to hold
divine service in Sadlers' Wells and other theatres and music
halls.[13] In all of this John Bird showed the same life-long
concern for the poor. Perhaps that concern was best exemplified
by the occasion when he went to one of the churches of his
diocese to give a sermon. On coming forward to the pulpit to
preach, he found a number of people standing in the aisles while
several pews were empty. He at once inquired the reason and
was told that the pews were private property and the owners
had shut them up. He immediately stopped the service and said:
'There can be no such thing in the house of God. Send for a
blacksmith to take off the locks. We will sing a hymn while he
does it.'[14]

Sumner's Concern for building Churches and Schools

In his early years, Sumner still shared the idealised notion of
previous generations that each parish church should have sufficient accommodation to seat all the inhabitants of the parish.
By the beginning of his time in Chester however, this was well
past being a practicable possibility in many industrial and inner
city parishes. Notwithstanding this, Sumner had an enduring
appetite and commitment to Church building on a grand scale.
In a period of rapid industrialisation and urbanisation, he saw
the overwhelming need for a Christian presence in each geographical locality. Whilst it was the case that not all the Church
buildings erected under his episcopate were appropriate in style

or size, the level of Christian life and commitment in the areas where they were built did increase significantly.[15] Sumner's concern for Church building was more than equalled by his concern for education. His vision was for a primary school in every parish. His enlightened views on teacher training and his vigorous support for the founding of Chester Training College were a major contribution to education in the north west of the country. It is a startling fact that during Sumner's time in Chester more than 700 schools were opened in the Diocese. John Bird saw a local school building not just as a place where Children could obtain a rudimentary education, but also as a centre where Christian meetings and other forms of instruction could take place. During his time in Canterbury, Sumner continued to promote school and church building, albeit on a rather less grandiose scale. He urged his clergy to take a strong lead in influencing the life and work of their parochial schools. K.S. Latourette in a terse summary of Sumner's achievements wrote: 'He stirred up his clergy to start day schools and Sunday Schools. To meet the needs of the mounting population he encouraged the erection of new churches and in 19 years consecrated 232 of them.'[16]

Sumner as a Defender of the Faith

William Gladstone wrote to Samuel Wilberforce in 1850 that it was not in the matter of their diocesan administration that he found fault with the bishops but rather in their defence of the Church's teaching in Parliament. Gladstone stated that 'although he was aware that there were some bishops who would stand firm to the Church's teaching, yet the great majority including the Archbishop, seemed utterly indifferent to upholding any dogmatic teaching in the Church'.[17] It is true that Sumner rarely spoke in Parliament on theological issues, preferring in the main to contribute to debates on social or moral issues. Nevertheless, of all the bishops of his generation, it could hardly be said of Sumner that he failed to contend for the faith of the Church. He stands out as one of the most forthright opponents of the Oxford movement in the 1840s and 50s. Yet the vigour of his attack against tractarian teaching and its later ritual innovations was a result not of any personal animus, but because he considered that it was set to undermine the fundamental Christian doctrine of justification by faith. Sumner held firm to the version of Anglicanism which he had inherited and which was shared by a great many of his contemporaries. He saw the *Thirty Nine Articles of Religion* and the liturgy of the *Book of Common Prayer* as the essential cornerstones of Anglicanism, and he was ready to draw on the insights of the Early Fathers of the undivided Catholic Church, only in so far as their teaching cohered with scripture. In all his replies to those who questioned him in matters of religious faith and practice from baptism to apostolic succession, Sumner's retort was the same: 'What do the Articles and the Book of Common Prayer permit us to believe on the matter?'

The intricacies of theological debate were by no means beyond the grasp of John Bird. He was one of the few prelates in 1848 who declined to sign Samuel Wilberforce's remonstrance against the appointment of Renn Hampden as Bishop of Hereford. He did so because after carefully scrutinising the text of Hampden's most recent writing he could not find the alleged departures from orthodox trinitarian theology. In the challenge posed by the publication of Charles Darwin's *Origin of Species* in 1859 Sumner was better equipped than most of his contemporaries. While his critic Samuel Wilberforce unleashed a storm of half-digested science and proclaimed fundamentalist interpretations of the early chapters of Genesis,[18] Sumner retained a quiet dignity. Indeed his enlightened views on the early chapters on Genesis were well in advance of those of his own generation.

Once again in his handling of the crisis which surrounded the publication of *Essays and Reviews* Sumner displayed the same characteristic restraint. He refrained from any immediate bombastic response of the kind made by Wilberforce or the more scholarly contributors to *Aids to Faith*.[19] When the heat had passed out of the debate, Sumner penned on behalf of the bishops a firm but guarded statement which was directed at the fundamental issues at stake. The *Record* commented of Sumner: 'It was felt that he was a safe man.... But on the other hand, he was no trimmer on questions affecting the great principles of Christ's gospel.'[20] The same article also paid tribute to Sumner's wise dealings with both the tractarians and the Gorham Case. It commented: 'Had Dr Phillpotts, or one or two other prelates who might be named, been elevated to the Primacy, the position of our Church would have been most perilous.'[21]

Sumner seems to have been one of those rare individuals who, like his master, spoke in such a way that 'all men wondered at the gracious words which proceeded out of his mouth'.[22] Perhaps his secret lay not only in his straightforward Christian walk but in the very practical rules by which he lived. Edward Benson, who later became Archbishop of Canterbury, gummed to the bottom of one of the drawers of his writing table where it could be seen every time it was open a rule of Sumner's. The strip of paper read as follows:

Rule
Never to answer for 24 hours any letters which in any account made his heart beat faster—asperities soften away, and my view of the writer's meaning gets so much fairer. Bp. Sumner[23]

In light of this it is no surprise that *The Saturday Review* in its obituary column gave fulsome praise to Sumner's ability of 'allaying the tempest' by his dignified gracious manner. It was to his great credit, the writer continued, that 'neither the Hampden Case, nor the Gorham Case, ever cost him an hour's sleep'.[24]

Setting a New Pattern of Episcopacy

Another of Sumner's enduring legacies was the manner in which he set a new pattern for episcopacy. Prior to Sumner's episcopate the average diocesan bishop was often a remote and lordly individual, who in many cases lived a life of ease, and in some instances one of princely splendour. Sumner was one of the first to emerge as a pastoral bishop and a man of the people. He was a great traveller who made a point of visiting his clergy, preaching for them and helping them in their efforts to raise funds. Sometimes he travelled round his diocese for two or three weeks at a time holding confirmations, encouraging, and visiting groups of churches in the locality. He took a particular interest in his clergy and their families. In his personal notes there are often scribbled lines about his incumbents' individual circumstances, or personal jottings about their wives or children. In his diocese John Bird was in a very real way a *Pastor Pastorum*.

In his efforts to support his clergy Sumner revamped the office of rural dean. As he envisaged this post, the rural dean was to be responsible for the clergy in his area, as well as for the Church and fabric. John Bird was always concerned about the low financial state of the clergy. Speaking at the bicentenary of the Sons of the Clergy Charity, he said that it was a matter of great regret that there should have been 'so much necessity for a charitable assistance'. Sumner also interested himself in the theological education of the clergy more than any other evangelical bishop. He was an active supporter of both St Bees College in Cumberland and St Aidan's College in Birkenhead.[25]

John Bird was the first Archbishop of Canterbury for many generations to be enthroned in person. He was also the first Archbishop of Canterbury whose revenues were diminished by a Parliamentary decree.[26] In his Canterbury Diocese even when he was well into his seventies Sumner continued to travel and visit his parishes with same earlier energy and vigour which he had shown in the Chester Diocese. R.C. Jenkins commented just a few years after his death:

> Few will fail to remember the energy and devotion with which up to the very last the archbishop entered upon all the duties which the care of the diocese devolved upon him. Up to his latest years he carried on his progress in the diocese, every part of which was known to him personally.[27]

In his journeyings, Sumner apparently travelled in the simplest manner with a single servant accompanying him.[28] Even as Archbishop of Canterbury, he still continued to live in the lifestyle of a quiet frugal country clergyman. He rose at dawn to pray, lit his own fire and dealt with most of the day's correspondence before breakfast. He refused to ride to the House of Lords in a state coach, but preferred instead to walk with his umbrella under his arm. In his later years at Lambeth and Addington, Sumner's unmarried daughter seems to have kept house for him. He valued the simple domestic pleasures and enjoyed the company of a small circle of close friends, among them Edward Hawke Locker, Henry Venn and William Marsh. He was essentially a private person who delighted in the company of his large family most of whom lived in the south-eastern counties in reasonably close proximity to the capital. Apart from his writing John Bird found relaxation in walking and in taking time out to engage in a little water-colour drawing.

Sumner as he was remembered by his Contemporaries

Sumner had many strengths. He was a fine scholar and wrote more than 30 books. Indeed it was said of him that he was one of the most fertile authors ever to be Archbishop of Canterbury. He was not without interest in learning and culture. Besides lending his hand to the founding of Chester Training College, and his active support of two theological Colleges, he was also a trustee of the British Museum. His detailed correspondence with Sir Anthony Panizzi (1797–1879), the Principal of the British Museum, indicates that he took an active interest in the Museum's collections and acquisitions.[29] Sumner read widely and enjoyed travel. He was a Privy Councillor, visitor of All Souls' and Merton Colleges, Oxford, King's College, London, St Augustine's College, Canterbury, Dulwich College School and Harrow School, the latter in conjunction with the Bishop of London. In addition he was President of the SPCK, the SPG and the National Society, and a Governor of Charterhouse School. On a wider stage he made a very positive contribution to the development of the rapidly growing Anglican Communion overseas. Yet when all this and more is said, it is significant that Sumner was universally remembered by his generation as a man of God. The *Record* summing up his life stated: '... the departed Primate was gifted with a combination of Christian graces which imparted a force and dignity to his character which it would not be easy to excel'.[30] In a funeral oration in Canterbury Dean Henry Alford spoke of their great thankfulness for 'the purity and unquestioned simplicity' of Sumner's

Christian faith and character. Towards the conclusion of the
same address the Dean commented: '... we knew his work was
safe for it was founded on the rock of personal piety: and that
his rule would be just because he ruled in the fear of God'.[31]
The *Times* also spoke of 'the justice of his rule', 'the holiness
of his life and the strength of his example'. 'In this view', the
paper continued, 'the late Archbishop must be regarded as one
of the best prelates that ever lived'.[32]

Perhaps the last words should come from the *Society for the
Promotion of Christian Knowledge* of which he was a life-long
supporter and advocate. At their meeting the month after Sumner's
death, the Standing Committee of SPCK proposed the following resolution of tribute which was unanimously adopted.

> We cannot but advert to the energy and success with which he
> laboured in the cause of Church Extension, and to the 300
> churches and chapels which he had the privilege of consecrating
> — to his numerous and valuable writings in support of Chris-
> tian truth, to the meek and gentleness which, in the administra-
> tion of his high office, marked his whole deprtment — to the
> bright example which he uniformly gave of domestic and social
> virtues, an example rendered more attractive by its unaffected
> simplicity — and to the wise moderation with which, at a
> critical period he was enabled by Providence to conduct the
> affairs of our National Church.[33]

Notes

1. See for example *The Saturday Review*, 13 September 1862; also *The
    Kentish Gazette* 16 September 1862.
2. *Times*, 8 September 1862, 10 September 1862.
3. Cave-Brown J., *Lambeth Palace and its Associations* (William
    Blackwood & Sons, 1883).
4. Baring-Gould S., *The Evangelical Revival* (Methuen, 1920), p. 265.
5. See Davidson R., *Five Archbishops: A sermon preached May 14,
    1911 by Randall, Archbishop of Canterbury on the occasion of the
    dedication of a Memorial Cross erected in Addington Churchyard*
    (London, SPCK, 1911), p.11.
6. See Liddon H.P., *Life of Edward Bouverie Pusey* (London, Long-
    man Green and Co., 1893) Vol. 1, p. 17.

7. Sumner J.B., *The Charge of John Bird, Lord Archbishop of Canterbury to the Clergy of the Diocese at His Primary Visitation* (London, J. Hatchard, 1849), p. 11.

8. Sumner J.B., *Charge to the Clergy of the Diocese of Chester* (London, J. Hatchard, 1829), p. 26.

9. *Ibid.*, p. 26.

10. See Sumner J.B., *A Charge delivered to the Clergy of the Diocese of Chester at His Triennial Visitation 1838* (London, J. Hatchard, 1838), p. 22.

11. Sumner J.B., *Charge* (1849), p. 11.

12. *Hansard*, Vol. CLI, February 1858.

13. *Hansard*, Vol. CLVI, 24 February 1860.

14. Balleine G.R., *A History of the Evangelical Party in the Church of England* (Longmans Green & Co., 1933), p. 195.

15. See chapter 4 which gives detailed coverage of Sumner's Chester episcopate and his church building activities.

16. Latourette K.S., *Christianity in a Revolutionary Age* (Paternoster, 1959), Vol. 2, p. 260.

17. Wilberforce R., *Life of Samuel Wilberforce* (John Murray, 1880–1882), Vol. 2, p. 130.

18. See Scotland N.A.D., '*Essays and Reviews* (1860) and the Reaction of Victorian Churches and Churchmen' in *The Downside Review*, April 1990, p. 151.

19. *Ibid.*, p. 154. See also Crowther M.A., *Church Embattled* (Newton Abbott, David and Charles, 1970), p. 167.

20. *Record*, 8 September 1862.

21. *Ibid.*

22. *Luke 4:22.*

23. Benson A.C., *The Life of Edward White Benson* (London, Macmillan & Co.,1899), Vol. 1, p. 613.

24. *Saturday Review*, 13 September 1862.

25. Crowther M.A., *op. cit.*, p. 234.

26. *The Illustrated London News*, 6 May 1848.

27. Jenkins R.C., *Diocesan Histories: Canterbury* (London, SPCK, 1880), p. 407.

28. Ibid., p. 407.

29. See Sumner's correspondence with Sir Anthony Panizzi British Museum MSS 36, 717, folios 420 & 581, MSS 36, 720, folio 81.

30. The *Record*, 8 September 1862.
31. *Kentish Gazette*, 16 September 1862.
32. *The Times*, 8 September 1862.
33. *SPCK Minute Book*, October 1862, pp. 484–485.

Select Bibliography

1. Writings by John Bird Sumner

Notebook (1804) (Cumbria Record Office).

Apostolic Preaching Considered in an Examination of St Paul's Epistles (1815).

A Treatise on the Records of the Creation and the Moral Attributes of the Creator (1816), 2 Vols.

'The Poor Laws', *British Review* (1817), Vol. 20, pp. 333–550.

The Encouragements of the Christian Minister (Aston and Henley, 1820).

A Series of Sermons on the Christian's Faith and Character (1821).

The Evidence of Creation (London, J. Hatchard, 1824).

Sermon preached at St Bride's Church Fleet Street on Monday Evening 2 May 1825 before the Church Missionary Society (London, J. Hatchard, 1825).

A Sermon Preached at Lambeth, 21 May 1826 at the Consecration of the Right Reverend Charles Sumner as Lord Bishop of Llandaff (Bodleian Library MS 28.534).

The Evidence of Christianity derived from its Nature and Reception (London, J. Hatchard, 1826).

Sermons on the Principal Festivals of the Church with Three Sermons on Good Friday (1827).

Four Sermons on Subjects relating to the Christian Ministry (London, 1828).

The Enlargement of Christ's Kingdom: A Sermon at Farnham Castle (London, 1828).

A Sermon Preached at St Mary's Church, Cambridge on Commencement Sunday 29 June 1828 and published by command of His Royal Highness Frederick Duke of Gloucester, Chancellor of the University (London, J. Hatchard & Son, 1828).

A Charge Delivered to the Clergy of the Diocese of Chester at the Primary Visitation in August and September 1829 (London, J. Hatchard, 1829).

A Letter to the Clergy of the Diocese of Chester, occasioned by the Act of the Legislature granting Relief to His Majesty's Roman Catholic Subjects (London, 1829).

A Charge Delivered to the Clergy of the Diocese of Chester at the Triennial Visitation in July and September 1832 (J. Hatchard, 1832).

Society for Promoting District Visiting: Fourth Annual Report and Sermon by the Bishop of Chester (1832).

A Charge Delivered to the Clergy of the Diocese of Chester at the Triennial Visitation in 1835 (London, J. Hatchard, 1835).

Notes on Parishes c. 1835 (Chester Diocesan Archives).

A Charge Delivered to the Clergy of the Diocese of Chester at the Triennial Visitation in 1838 (London, J. Hatchard, 1838).

Eternal Life in Jesus Christ: A Sermon preached at the Consecration of St Luke's Church, Cheetham Hill (London and Chester, 1840).

Christian Charity: Its Obligations and Objects With Reference to the Present State of Society (London, J. Hatchard, 1841).

A Charge Delivered to the Clergy of the Diocese of Chester in 1841 (London, J. Hatchard & Son, 1841).

The Doctrine of Justification Briefly Stated (London, J. Hatchard & Son, 1843).

A Practical Exposition of Paul to the Romans (London, , J. Hatchard & Son,1843.

A Charge Addressed to the Clergy of the Dioceses of Chester at the Triennial Visitation in May and June 1844 (London, J. Hatchard, 1844).

Act Books Vols. 1 and 2, 1848–62 (Lambeth Palace Library).

Regeneration in Baptism and Apostolic Doctrine (1849).

The Charge of John Bird, Lord Archbishop of Canterbury, to the Clergy of the Diocese at his Primary Visitation (London, J. Hatchard, 1849).

A Sermon Preached on Jeremiah xxxi.34 for the Society for Promoting Christian Knowledge (SPCK, Annual Report, 1849).

Anniversary Sermon Preached 5 June 1851, for the Society for Promoting Christian Knowledge (Annual Report, 1851).

A Sermon Preached at the Metropolitan Cathedral of St Paul on the Occasion of the Jubilee of the British and Foreign Bible Society on Wednesday 9 March 1853 (Seeleys, 1853).

The Charge of John Bird Lord Archbishop of Canterbury to the Clergy of the Diocese at His Visitation 1853 (London, J. Hatchard & Son, 1853).

The Christian's Dependence upon his Redeemer (Edinburgh, James Hogg & Sons, 1857).

The Charge of John Bird Lord Archbishop of Canterbury to the Clergy of the Diocese at His Visitation 1857 (London, J. Hatchard, 1857).

A Charge Delivered at the Confirmation of the Prince of Wales, April 1858 printed by His Majesty's Command.

Marriage with Deceased Wife's Sister: The Speech of the Archbishop of Canterbury and Other Authorities, Ancient and Modern, on Marriage with a Deceased Wife's Sister (London, 1859).

Practical Reflections on Select Passages in the New Testament (London, J. Hatchard & Sons, 1859).

2. Unpublished Sources

Aberdeen Papers. Vol. CLVII.

Baptismal Register Parish of Kenilworth, MS DR/101 1763–
1778, DR/10/S 1779–1812.

Boveney Chapel Wardens' Account Book BCRO MS PR
72/5/1.

Canterbury Acts of Consecration (CDA) 1841–48; 1848–55;
1855–60; 1860–69.

Canterbury Diocesan Faculties 1754–1854 (CDA)

Canterbury National Schools' Minute Book (CDA) MS
U/9/F/1.

Chester City Council Assembly Book (CCA) Assembly Book
6.

Chester Diocesan SPCK Minute Book (CCA) MS EDD1/18.

*Chester District Association for the Society of the Propagation
of the Gospel 1831–1881* (CCA) MS EDD1/19.

Church Missionary Society Letter Books (Birmingham Univer-
sity Library) North India (C11); West India (C13); South
India (C12); Sierra Leone (CA1); Yoruba (CA2), China (C
CH), New Zealand (C N); North West America (C C1),
Mauritius (CMA); Correspondence with British Isles
(G/AC1).

Church Pastoral Aid Society Committee Reports.

Deed of two Cottages sold to Revd Robert Sumner, 1787 DR
189/1 5/7B (WCA).

Duncombe D., *A List of the Number of Churches Consecrated
in Each Year in the Diocese of Chester from 1801–1871*
(CRO).

Ellenborough Papers PRO Ref. 27/3 at Kew).

Eton Register of Christenings 1748–1810 (BCRO) PR 72/1/4Q.

Eton Register of Christenings 1813–1839 PR 72/1/1/9Q. *Eton
Register of Marriages 1813–37* MS PR 72/1/14.

Festival of the Sons of the Clergy 1848–57 (Canterbury Cathedral Archives) MS 31947–8.

General Society for Promoting District Visiting British Museum MS 4765d+21).

Gladstone Correspondence, British Museum MS 44358, 44359.

The Earl Grey Papers (3rd Earl), University of Durham, Dept of Palaeography and Diplomatic.

Bishop's Act Books 1825–35 (EDA 11/11 Chester Diocesan Archives).

Bishop's Act Books 1835–40 (EDA 1/12 Chester Diocesan Archives).

Bishop's Registers 1821–32, 1831–37, 1838–45, 1845–47, 1847–50, 1848–54 (EDA 2 Chester Diocesan Archives).

Liverpool Papers (British Museum MS 38, 301, folio 181).

Locker Papers (Huntingdon Library, San Marino, California, USA).

Longley Papers 1811–45 (LPL).

Madden Papers (British Museum MS Eg 2846).

Mapledurham Parish Records (OCRO) *Register of Baptisms 1813–67* MS 61; *Register of Marriages 1813–37* MS 62; *Overseers' Accounts 1805–31* MS 64; *Accounts of Poor Rates 1814–35* MS E2; *Vicarial Tithe Records 1086–1677* MS C4; *Accounts and Surveys of the Highways* MS E3; *Church Wardens' and Overseers' Accounts* MS C2A/C.

New Windsor Parish Records (BCRO) *Register of Marriages 1801–1812* DP MF 970281/6; *Register of Marriages 1813–37* DP MF 97028 1/7; *Register of Baptisms 1813–27* DP MF 10308 1/17; *Register of Charity Sermons in Windsor Parish Church 1785–1879* 18/1; *Church Wardens' Accounts 1798–1813* DP 149/MF 10149; *General Register 1773–1825* DP 149 8/1.

Panizzi Correspondence (British Museum MS 36,717; 36,720).

Peel Papers (British Museum MS 40,412 Volumes CCLXII; CCLXXI; CCLXXIV; CCCLXXXV; CCCXC; CCCXCII; CCCXCIII; CCCVI; CCCCVII; CCCCXIII).

Russell Papers (PRO) 8659 MS 5C 230/231; *Lord John Russell Letter Book 1847–51* (MS ENG LETTERS d307).
SPCK Minute Books.
SPG Annual Reports.
Tait Papers (LPL).

3. Newspapers and Periodicals

British Magazine.
Chester Chronicle.
Chester Diocesan Gazette.
Christian Observer.
Church of England Magazine.
Church Guardian.
Church Times.
Contemporary Review.
Chronicle of Convocation.
Edinburgh Review.
Eton and Windsor Express.
Gentleman's Magazine.
Hansard 1829–62.
Illustrated London News.
Journals of the House of Lords.
Kentish Gazette.
Manchester Guardian.
Quarterly Review.
The Record.
The Times.

4. Books and Articles

Alford F., *Life, Journal and Letters of Henry Alford DD* (Rivingtons, London, 1873).
Anon, *Etoniana, and Ancient and Modern* (William Blackwood, Edinburgh, 1865).

Ashwell A.R. and Wilberforce R.G., *Life of the Right Reverend Samuel Wilberforce* (John Murray, 1880–82) III Vols.

Balleine G.P., *A History of the Evangelical Party* (Longman's, 1933).

Baring-Gould S., *The Evangelical Revival* (Methuen, 1920).

Bayfield Roberts G., *The History of the English Church Union 1859–94* (London Church Printing Company, 1898).

Beavan A.B., *The Aldermen of the City of London* (London, 1908) 2 Vols.

Bebbington D.W., *Evangelicalism in Modern Britain* (Unwin Hyman, 1989).

Benson A.C., *Fasti Etonenses: A Biographical History of Eton* (London, Simpkin, Marshall & Co., 1899).

Benson A.C., *The Life of Edward White Benson* 2 Vols. (London Macmillan & Co., 1899).

Best G.F.A., *Temporal Pillars* (CUP, 1964).

Birks T.R., *A Memoir of the Rev Edward Bickersteth* 2 Vols. (London, Seeleys, 1853).

Blomfield A.F. (ed.), *A Memoir of Charles James Blomfield* 2 Vols. (John Murray, 1863).

Bowen D., *The Idea of the Victorian Church 1833–89* (Montreal, McGill University Press, 1968).

Bradbury J.L., *Chester College and the Training of Teachers 1839–75* (Chester College, 1975).

Brose O., *Church and Parliament 1828–60* (Stanford University Press, 1959).

Brown F.K., *Fathers of the Victorians: The Age of Wiberforce* (CUP,1961).

Carus W. (ed.), *Memoirs of the Life of the Rev. Charles Simeon MA* (Hatchard, 1848).

Cave-Brown J., *Lambeth Palace and its Associations* (William Blackwood & Sons, 1883).

Church R.W., *The Oxford Movement 1833–45* (London, Macmillan, 1900).

Combs J., *George and Mary Sumner* (The Sumner Press, 1965).

Crowther M.A., *Church Embattled* (Newton Abbott, David & Charles, 1970).

Cust L., *History of Eton College* (London, Duckworth, 1899).

Danks W., *Memoirs of the Cathedral and Priory Church in Canterbury* (London, Chapman, 1912).

Davidson R.T. & Benham W., *Life of Archbishop Campbell Tait*, 2 Vols. (London, Macmillan, 1891).

Davidson R.T., *Five Archbishops: A Sermon Preached May 14 1911 by Randall, Archbishop of Canterbury, on the Occasion of the Dedication of a Memorial Cross erected in Addington to Churchyard* (London, SPCK, 1911).

Davies G.C.B., *Henry Phillpotts Bishop of Exeter 1778–1869* (SPCK, 1954).

Davies G.C.B., *Men for the Ministry* (Hodder, 1963).

Elliot-Binns L., *The Evangelical Movement in the English Church* (Methuen, 1928).

Flindall R.P., *The Church of England 1815–48* (London, SPCK, 1972).

Fowler M., *Some Notable Archbishops of Canterbury* (London, SPCK, 1895).

Gardener's Gazetteer and Directory of the County of Oxford (Gardener, 1852).

Gilbert A.D., *Religion and Society in Industrial England* (Longman, 1976).

Gill R., *The Myth of the Empty Church* (SPCK, 1993).

Hammond P., *The Parson and the Victorian Parish* (Hodder & Stoughton, 1977).

Heginbotham H., *Stockport Ancient and Modern* (Simpson, Low, Searle & Rivington, 1882).

Hennell M., *Sons of the Prophets* (London, SPCK, 1979).

Hibbert L., *George IV Regent and King* (Allen Lane, 1974).

Hilton B., *The Age of Atonement* (Clarendon, 1988).

Jenkins R.C., *Diocesan Histories: Canterbury* (London, SPCK, 1880).

Jesse J.H., *Memoirs of Celebrated Etonians* (London, J.C. Nimmo, 1881).

Kirwan-Browne E.G., *Annals of the Tractarian Movement 1842–60* (London, private publisher, 1861).

Kitchen G.W., *Edward Harold Browne Lord Bishop of Winchester* (London, J. Murray, 1895).

Lathbury D.C., *Correspondence on Church and Religion of William Ewart Gladstone*, 2 Vols. (London, J. Murray, 1910).

Latourette K.S., *Christianity in a Revolutionary Age* (Paternoster Press, 1959).

Lewis D.M., *Lighten Their Darkness* (Greenwood Press, 1986).

Liddon H.P., *Life of Edward Bouverie Pusey*, 4 Vols. (London, Longman, Green & Co., 1893).

Loane M., *Hewn from the Rock* (Sydney, 1976).

Loane M., *John Charles Ryle 1816–1900* (Hodder, 1983).

Lyte M., *A History of Eton College 1440–1910* (Macmillan & Co., 1911).

Marsden J.B., *Memoirs of the Life and Labours of the Rev. Hugh Stowell* (Hamilton Adams & Co, 1865).

Massingberd F.C., *The Necessity of a Session of Convocation* (London, F.J. Rivington, 1850).

Morris R.H., *Diocesan Histories: Chester* (London, SPCK, 1895).

Morse-Boycott D., *The Second Story of the Oxford Movement* (London, Skeffington & Son, 1933).

Moule H.G.C., *Charles Simeon* (IVP, 1956).

Moule H.G.C., *The Evangelical School in the Church of England* (London, 1901).

Mozley A., *Lectures and Correspondence from Henry Newman* 2 Vols. (London, Longman, Green & Co., 1891).

Norman E.R., *Christianity in the Southern Hemisphere* (Clarendon, 1981).

Newsome D., *The Parting of Friends* (John Murray, 1966).

Overton J.H., *The Anglican Revival* (London, Blackie & Son, 1897).

Palmer A., *The Life and Times of George IV* (Weidenfeld and Nicholson, 1972).

Palmer W., *A Narrative of Events Connected with the Publication of Tracts for the Times* (London, Rivingtons, 1883).

Pascoe C.F., *Two Hundred Years of SPG 1701–1900* (London, SPG, 1901).

Phillpotts H., *Letter to the Archbishop of Canterbury from the Bishop of Exeter* (London, J. Murray, 1850).

Pollard A., 'Evangelical Clergy 1820–1840', *Church Quarterly Review 1958*, Vol. 159.

Reynolds J.S., *Canon Christopher of St Aldates* (Abbey Press, Abingdon, 1967).

Reynolds J.S., *The Evangelicals at Oxford* (Marcham Manor, 1975).

Roberts G., *A Plain Tract showing the History and Nature of Convocation* (London, F.J. Rivington, 1850).

Russell A., *The Clerical Profession* (London, SPCK, 1980).

Russell G.W.E., *A Short History of the Evangelical Movement* (Mowbray, 1915).

Shephard V., *Old Days of Eton Sareth* (Spottiswoode & Co., 1908).

Simeon C., *Let Wisdom Judge: University Addresses and Sermons* (IVP, 1959).

Slade J., *A Memoir of the Rev. Canon James Slade* (1892).

Smyth C., *Simeon and Church Order* (Cambridge, 1940).

Smyth C. 'The Evangelical Movement in Perspective', *Cambridge Historical Journal* 1943, Vol 7.

Soloway R.A., *Prelates and People* (Routledge & Kegan Paul, 1969).

Sterry W. *Annals of King's College and of Our Lady of Eton Beside Windsor* (London, Methuen, 1908).

Stewart D.D., *Memoir of the Life of the Rev. James Stewart* (London, Hatchard, 1857).

Stock E., *The English Church in the Nineteenth Century* (London, Longman, Green & Co, 1910).

Stock E., *The History of the Church Missionary Society*, 3 Vols. (London, CMS, 1899).

Stoldant A.M., *The Life of Isabella Bird* (London, John Murray, 1908).

Sumner G.H., *Life of R. C. Sumner DD, Bishop of Winchester* (John Murray, 1872).

Tagg J., *Revival of Convocation: An Address before East Bethnall Green Church Union* (London, Wertheim & MacIntosh, 1850).

Thompson H.P., *Into All Lands: The History of the Society of the Gospel in Foreign Parts 1901–1950* (London, SPCK, 1851).

Walsh W., *The History of the Romeward Movement in the Church of England 1833–64* (London, James Wisbet & Co., 1900).

Ward W.R., *Religion and Society in England 1790–1850* (London, B.T. Batsford Lt, 1972).

Waterman A.M.C., 'The Ideological Alliance of Political Economy and Christian Theology 1798–1833', *Journal of Ecclesiastical History*, Vol. 34, No. 2, April 1983.

Waterman A.M.C., *Revolution, Economics and Religion* (CUP, 1991).

Weldon J.E.C., *Recollections and Reflections* (London, Cassell & Co., 1915).

Westbury Jones J., *Figgis of Brighton* (London, Paternoster Press, 1917).

Wilkinson C.A., *Reminiscences of Eton* (London, Hurst and Blackett Ltd., 1888).

Yates N., *Kent and the Oxford Movement* (Kent Archives Office, 1983).

Appendix

People who kindly gave help and advice in a variety of ways

Dr David Bebbington, Reader in History at Stirling University.

Mr E.W. Bill, Librarian, Lambeth Palace Library.

Mr David J. Brown, Scottish Record Office.

Mr D.J Butley, County Archivist, Durham County Council.

Mr R.J.E. Bush, Deputy County Archivist, Somerset Records Office.

Miss C.F. Cattermole, Archives Assistant, Hampshire Record Office.

Miss Pamela Clark, Royal Archives, Windsor Castle.

Mrs Shirley Corke, County Archivist, Surrey County Council.

D. Crook, Search Department, Public Record Office.

Mr C.R. Davey, County Records Officer, East Sussex.

Mr M.W. Farr, Warwick County Archivist.

Canon John Grimwade QC, Priest-in-Charge, Stonesfield.

Miss Susan Hare, Librarian, Goldsmith's Hall, London.

Mrs Penelope Hatfield, Archivist, Eton College.

Canon Michael Hennell, formerly Principal of Ridley Hall, Cambridge.

Dr Michael Halls, Modern Archivist, King's College, Cambridge.

N.W. James, Research Assistant, Royal Commission on Historical Manuscripts.

M. Joyce, Reference Librarian, Bath Reference Library.

Dr G.A. Knight, Principal Archivist, Lincolnshire County Council.

Dr Peter Linehan, St John's College, Cambridge.

Mr Anthony Malcolmson, Archivist, Public Record Office of Northern Ireland.

Miss Sheila MacPherson, County Archivist, Cumbria County Council.

Miss M.S. McCollum, Assistant Keeper, Dept of Palaeography, University of Durham.

Mr R.C. Norris, Special Collections, University of Durham.

Miss A.M. Oakley, Archivist, Cathedral City & Diocesan Records Office.

Revd J.S. Reynolds.

Mr K.H. Rogers, County Archivist, Wiltshire County Record Office.

James R. Sewell, City Archivist, City of London.

Mrs June Smith, Assistant Librarian, Ridley Hall.

Mr Cecil Sumner.

Mr Jeffery Turner.

Dr John Wolfe, Open University.

Miss F.S. Wright, Assistant Librarian, The Evangelical Library.

Genealogy

Table 1.

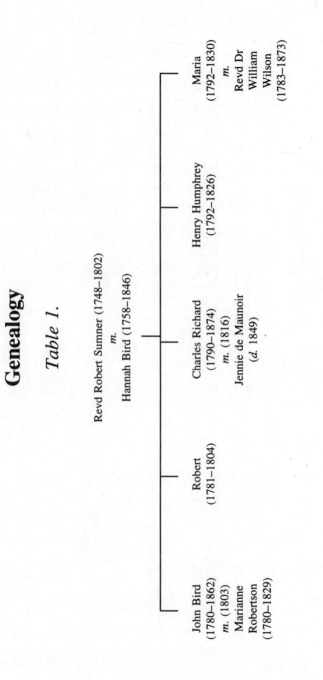

Revd Robert Sumner (1748–1802)
m.
Hannah Bird (1758–1846)

John Bird
(1780–1862)
m. (1803)
Marianne
Robertson
(1780–1829)

Robert
(1781–1804)

Charles Richard
(1790–1874)
m. (1816)
Jennie de Maunoir
(*d.* 1849)

Henry Humphrey
(1792–1826)

Maria
(1792–1830)
m.
Revd Dr
William
Wilson
(1783–1873)

Table 2.

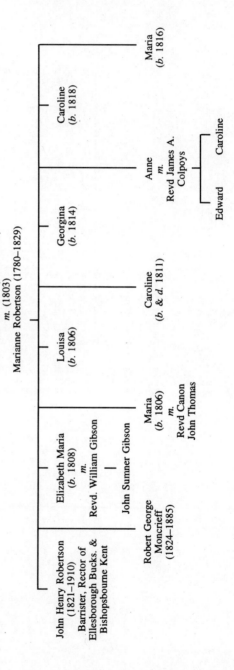

Index

Holy Spirit
  in confirmation 115
  in evangelicalism 95
Hook, Walter Farquhar 151
Hope, Beresford 127
Hopkins, Bishop of Vermont
  139–40
Howley, William, death xii, 111
human nature, corruption 17, 85

Illustrated London News 103, 113
immmigration, from Ireland 46,
  67, 114
Incorporated Society 126
India, government 77
indigence, and poverty 21–2, 23
industrialisation
  effects xi, xii, 21, 154
  in Lancashire 46
Ireland
  emigration from 46, 67, 114
  and importation of Irish
    clergy 52, 91
  and Sumner 37

Jenkins, R.C. 128
Jowett, Benjamin 122
justification
  and crucicentrism 96
  by faith 17–18, 84–8, 112, 156
  and works 82, 85–7

Keate, John (head master of
  Eton) 6, 12–13
Keble, John
  and Oxford Movement 81, 82
  and St Augustine's College
    127
Kenilworth, and Sumner's fam-
  ily 1–4, 9–10
King, Lord 71
King's College, Cambridge

and Eton 11
  Sumner at 5–6, 98
  Sumner family connections 1
King's College, London 159
Kingsley, Charles 151
Kinnaird, Arthur 135

Lambeth Conferences, development 139–40, 148
Lancashire
  and church-building xii, 48,
    49–50
  population 46, 48
  and Roman Catholicism 67
Lancashire Visiting Society 56
Lancaster, use of lay visitors 54–
  5
Latourette, K.S. 155
Law, George, Bishop of Chester
  47
law, secular, and Church of England 74, 116
laymen
  in colonial Church 75–6
  as visitors 53–6, 60, 105
Legg, Edward, Bishop of Oxford
  30
Lewis, Francis 9
Liverpool
  and church-building 48
  and industrialisation 46
  Irish immigrants 67, 91
  living conditions 46
Liverpool diocese, creation 47
Locker, Edward Hawke 38, 40,
  78 n.5, 159
London City Mission 56
Longley, C.T., Bishop of Ripon
  111–12
Lonsdale, John, Bishop of Lichfield 112